FLOYD CLYMER'S BOOK OF THE S.U. CARBURETOR

INTRODUCTION

Welcome to the world of digital publishing ~ the book you now hold in your hand, while unchanged from the original publication, was printed using the latest state of the art digital technology. The advent of print-on-demand has forever changed the publishing process, never has information been so accessible and it is our hope that this book serves your informational needs for years to come. If this is your first exposure to digital publishing, we hope that you are pleased with the results. Many more titles of interest to the classic automobile and motorcycle enthusiast, collector and restorer are available via our website at www.VelocePress.com. We hope that you find this title as interesting as we do.

NOTE FROM THE PUBLISHER

The information presented is true and complete to the best of our knowledge. All recommendations are made without any guarantees on the part of the author or the publisher, who also disclaim all liability incurred with the use of this information.

TRADEMARKS

We recognize that some words, model names and designations, for example, mentioned herein are the property of the trademark holder. We use them for identification purposes only. This is not an official publication.

INFORMATION ON THE USE OF THIS PUBLICATION

In today's information age we are constantly subject to changes in common practice, new technology, availability of improved materials and increased awareness of chemical toxicity. As such, it is advised that the user consult with an experienced professional prior to undertaking any procedure described herein. While every care has been taken to ensure correctness of information, it is obviously not possible to guarantee complete freedom from errors or omissions or to accept liability arising from such errors or omissions. Therefore, any individual that uses the information contained within, or elects to perform or participate in do-it-yourself repairs or modifications acknowledges that there is a risk factor involved and that the publisher or its associates cannot be held responsible for personal injury or property damage resulting from the use of the information or the outcome of such procedures.

It is important that the reader recognizes that any instructions may refer to either the right-hand or left-hand sides of the vehicle or the components and that the directions are followed carefully. One final word of advice, this publication is intended to be used as a reference guide, and when in doubt the reader should consult with a qualified technician.

CONTENTS

Compiled and updated from the two **Floyd Clymer** books, **'Handbook of Imported Carburetors & Fuel Injection'** and **'B.M.C. Mini Cars Handbook'**, this publication is specific to the **H, HS** and **HD** series of SU carburetors, specifically the **H1, H2, HS2, H4, HS4, H6, HS6, HD6 & HD8** types.

It is important for the reader to remember that the data was extracted from books published in the mid 1960's, so the information it contains is relevant to that date. However, as this series of SU carburetors was in production for almost 30 years after the publication dates, much of the information it contains is applicable to those same SU carburetors that were fitted to later makes and models of automobiles. Therefore, while some minor differences in mounting and linkage may occur, the same adjustment and tuning data can be applied.

Consequently, for the sake of simplification, this book focuses on five popular single, twin and triple SU carburetor installations (1) Austin Healey 'Big Healey's' (2) Austin Healey Sprite & Midgets (3) Austin Mini & Mini Cooper (4) Jaguar XKE & MK10 and (5) Volvo. However, there is a cross reference included in the index under each of those installations that identifies some, but certainly not all, other applicable makes and models that utilize the same, or similar, carburetors.

The book is split into sections, the first section includes a 'how to' identify the type of SU carburetor, design and operational information, overhaul and adjustments. The second section is applicable to the different SU carburetor types covered in detail in the later sections of the book and includes information on tuning and synchronizing. The remaining sections identify the five major installations referenced above.

We believe this book is an important addition to any automotive enthusiast's library and will help keep their SU Carburetor equipped automobiles in top operating condition.

SECTION INDEX

(1) SU CARBURETORS (General) - Identification, design, operation, overhaul & adjustments.

(2) SU CARBURETORS - Tuning & synchronizing

(3) AUSTIN HEALEY 'BIG HEALEY's' H4, H6, HD6, HS4 & HS6
Both 4 & 6 cylinder models (1953 - Onwards)

Data is also applicable to:
Austin Healey Sprite & Midget (1498cc engines)	HS4
B.M.C. 1300's - 1300cc Clubman etc.	HS4 & HS6
MGA & MGB (1955 - Onwards)	H4 & HS4
Jaguar XK120, XK140, XK150 (1948 – Onwards)	H6 & HD6
Jaguar MK VII, MKVIII & MKIX (1950 – Onwards)	H6 & HD6
Jaguar 240, 3.4 MK1 & MK2, 3.8 MK2 (1967 – Onwards)	HS6 & HD6
Jaguar 3.4 & 3.8 S Type (1963 – Onwards)	HD6
Rover 3500 (1968-1970)	HS6
Triumph TR2, TR3 & TR4 (1953 – Onwards)	H4 & H6
See Main Volvo Section for additional details on	H4 & HS6

(4) AUSTIN HEALEY SPRITE MK1, MK2 & MG MIDGET
948cc, 1098cc & 1275cc. (1958 - Onwards) H1 & HS2

Data is also applicable to:
Morris Minor (800cc Engine)	H1

(5) AUSTIN MINI & MINI COOPER
850cc, 997cc, 998cc, 1071cc & 1275cc (1959 – Onwards) HS2

Data is also applicable to:
B.M.C. Mini's – Austin, Morris, Riley etc. (1959 – Onwards)	HS2
B.M.C 1100's & some 1300's (1962 – Onwards)	HS2
Morris Minor 1000 (1098cc Engine)	HS2

(6) JAGUAR XKE & MKX HD8
3.8 & 4.2 (1961 – Onwards)

Data is also applicable to:
Jaguar XK150S 3.4 & 3.8(1958-1960) & 420 (1966-1968)	HD8

(7) VOLVO
(Engine B14A) H2
(Engines) B16B, B18B & B18D (1961-1968) H4 & HS6

Data is also applicable to:
Morris Minor (948cc Engine)	H2
Triumph Spitfire (1147cc & 1296 cc Engines)	H2

PAGE INDEX

SECTION 1 - PAGE 1

(1) SU CARBURETORS (General) - Identification, design, operation, overhaul & adjustments.

SECTION 2 - PAGE 18

(2) SU CARBURETORS - Tuning & synchronizing

SECTION 3 - PAGE 27

(3) AUSTIN HEALEY 'BIG HEALEY's' H4, H6, HD6, HS4 & HS6
Both 4 & 6 cylinder models (1953 - Onwards)

SECTION 4 - PAGE 48

(4) AUSTIN HEALEY SPRITE MK1, MK2 & MG MIDGET
948cc, 1098cc & 1275cc. (1958 - Onwards) H1 & HS2

SECTION 5 - PAGE 63

(5) AUSTIN MINI & MINI COOPER
850cc, 997cc, 998cc, 1071cc & 1275cc (1959 – Onwards) HS2

SECTION 6 - PAGE 70

(6) JAGUAR XKE & MKX HD8
3.8 & 4.2 (1961 – Onwards)

SECTION 7 - PAGE 91

(7) VOLVO
(Engine B14A) H2
(Engines) B16B, B18B & B18D (1961-1968) H4 & HS6

S.U. CARBURETORS TYPES & IDENTIFICATION

Type H – First introduced 1937

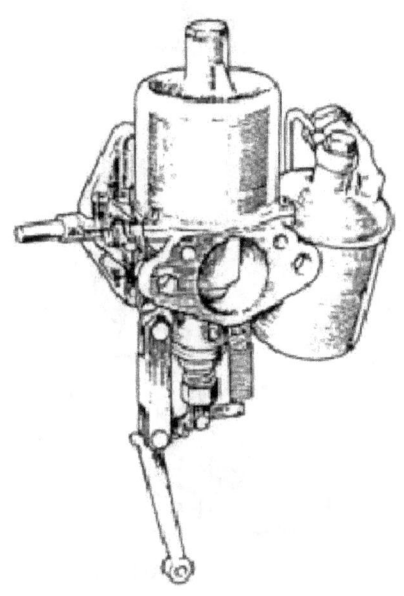

IDENTIFIED BY: The float bowl has an arm cast into its base, which mounts to the bottom of the carburetor with a hollow bolt or banjo fitting. Fuel passes through the arm into the carburetor body. The bolt attaches to the carburetor body just behind the main jet assembly. There is also a brass lever to the bottom of the carburetor that operates the jet.

Available in 5 sizes:

H1 1 1/8" = 28.58mm - early Morris Minor & AH Sprite etc.

H2 1 2/8" = 31.75mm - early Volvo & some Triumph Spitfires etc.

H4 1 4/8" = 38.10mm - early Triumph TR's, MGA, Big Healey etc.

H6 1 6/8" = 44.45mm - early Jaguar XK's, MK VII, VII, IX etc.

H8 1 8/8" = 50.80mm - primarily competition & high performance use.

Type HD – First introduced 1954

Retaining Screws

IDENTIFIED BY: The float bowl mounted with its arm fastening directly below, and concentric with, the main jet. The arm has a flange that fastens with 4 screws to the bottom of the carburetor, and sealed with a rubber diaphragm integral with the main jet.

Available in 3 sizes:

HD4 1 4/8" = 38.10 mm - MG Magnette etc.

HD6 1 6/8" = 44.45 mm - Big Healey's & Jaguars etc.

HD8 1 8/8" = 50.80 mm - Jaguar, 420, XKE, MKX etc.

Type HS – First introduced in 1958

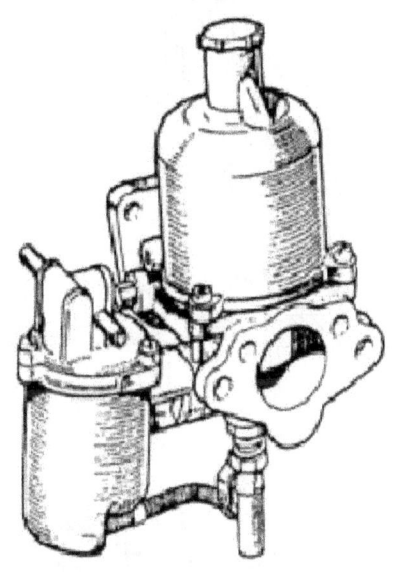

IDENTIFIED BY: The float bowl rigidly mounted to the carburetor body, the fuel is transferred by a separate external flexible line from the bottom of the float bowl to the jet assembly.

Available in 4 sizes:

HS2 1 2/8" = 31.75mm - early Mini's, Morris Minor, BL 1100's etc.

HS4 1 4/8" = 38.10mm - Big Healey's, BL 1300's, MGB etc

HS6 1 6/8" = 44.45mm - Jaguar, Triumph TR's, Volvo, Rover 3500 etc.

HS8 1 8/8" = 50.80mm - Primarily competition & high performance use.

S.U. CARBURETORS

NOTE: The identification numbers on the cutaway drawing below are referred to in the description which follows.

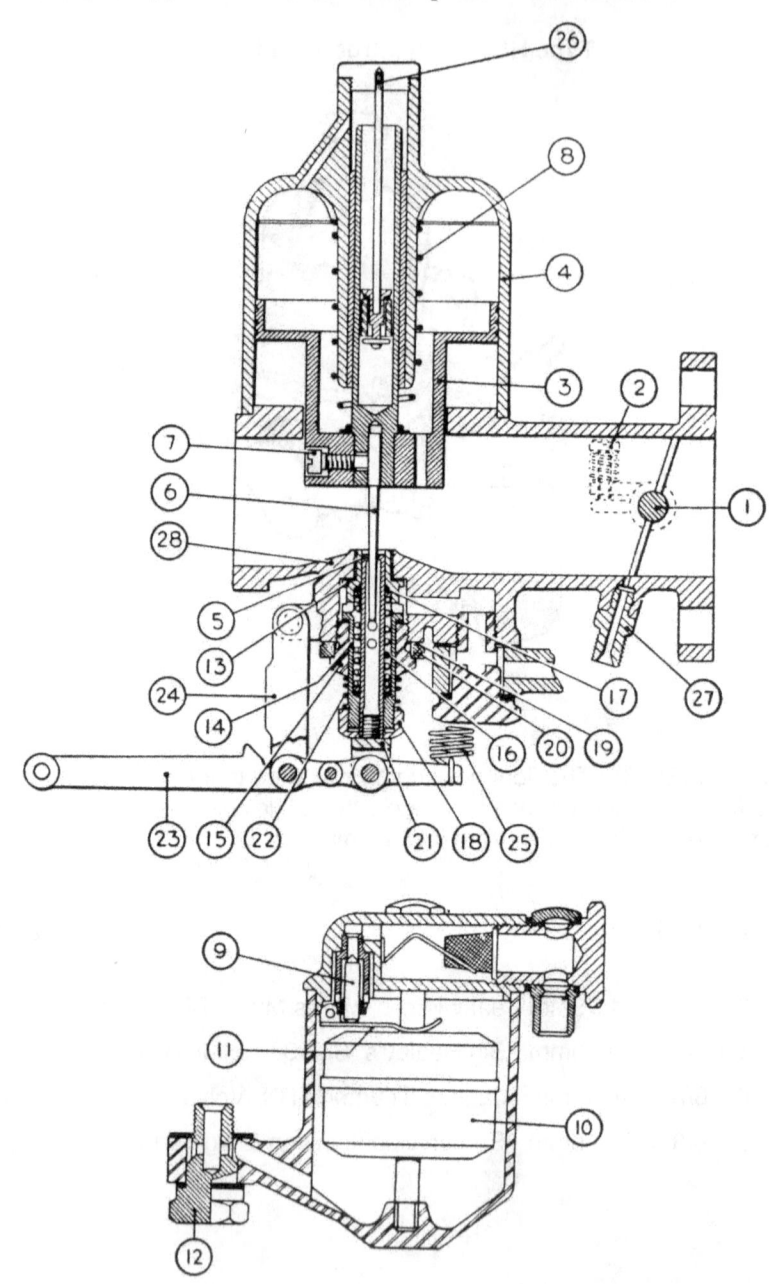

Description

The S.U. carburetor is of the automatically expanding choke type, in which the cross sectional area of the main air passage adjacent to the fuel jet, and the effective orifice of the jet, is variable. The variation takes place in accordance with the demand of the engine as determined by the degree of the throttle opening, the engine speed, and the load against which the engine is operating.

The distinguishing feature of the type of carburetor is that an approximately constant air velocity, and hence an approximately constant degree of depression, is at all times maintained in the region of the fuel jet. This velocity is such that the air flow demanded by the engine in order to develop its maximum power is not appreciably impeded, although good atomization of the fuel is assured under all conditions of speed and load.

The maintenance of a constant high air velocity across the jet, even under idling conditions, obviates the necessity for an idling jet. A single jet only is employed in the S.U. carburetor.

Construction

The main constructional features of the carburetor in its simplest form are shown in the accompanying drawings, which illustrate the horizontal-type carburetor. The diagrams illustrate the main body, butterfly throttle, automatically expanding choke and variable fuel-jet arrangement. They also indicate the means whereby the jet is lowered by a manual control to effect enrichment of the mixture for starting and warming up.

It will be seen that a butterfly throttle mounted on the spindle (1) is located close to the engine attachment flange, at one end of the main air passage, and that an adjustable idling stop screw (2) is arranged to prevent complete closure of the throttle, thus regulating the flow of mixture from the carburetor under idling conditions with the accelerator released. At the outer end of the main passage is mounted the piston (3), its lower part constituting a shutter, restricting the cross-sectional area of the main air passage in the vicinity of the fuel jet (5) as the piston falls. This component is enlarged at its upper end to form a piston of considerably greater diameter which moves axially within the bore of the suction chamber (4) and at the bottom of the piston is mounted the tapered needle (6) which is retained by means of the setscrew (7).

The piston component (3) is carried upon a central spindle which reciprocates and is mounted in a bush fitted in the central boss, forming the upper part of the suction chamber casting.

An extremely accurate fit is provided between the spindle and the bush in the suction chamber so that the enlarged portion of the piston is held out of contact with the bore of the suction chamber, within which, nevertheless, it operates with an extremely fine clearance. Similarly, the needle (6) is restrained from contacting the bore of the jet (5) which it is seen to penetrate, moving axially therein to correspond with the rise and fall of the piston.

It will be appreciated that, as the piston rises, the air passage in the neighborhood of the jet becomes enlarged, and passes an additional quantity of air. Provided that the needle (6) is of a suitably tapered form, its simultaneous withdrawal from the jet (5) ensures the delivery to the engine of the required quantity of fuel corresponding to any given position of the piston and hence to a given air flow.

The piston, under the influence of its own weight and assisted by the light compression spring (8) will tend to occupy its lowest position, two slight protuberences on its lower face contacting the bottom surface of the main air passage adjacent to the jet. The surface in this region is raised somewhat above the general level of the main bore of the carburetor, and is referred to as the "bridge" (28).

Levitation of the piston is achieved by means of the induction depression, which takes effect within the suction chamber, and thus upon the upper surface of the enlarged portion of the piston through drillings in the lower part of the piston which make communication between this region and that lying between the piston and the throttle. The annular space beneath the enlarged portion of the piston is completely vented to atmosphere by ducts not indicated in the diagram.

It will be appreciated that, since the weight of the piston assembly is constant, and the augmenting load of the spring (8) approximately so, a substantially constant degree of depression will prevail within the suction chamber, and consequently in the region between the piston and the throttle, for any given degree of lift of the piston between the extremities of its travel.

It will be clear that this floating condition of the piston will be stable for any given airflow demand as imposed by the degree of throttle opening, the engine speed and the load; thus, any tendency in the piston to fall momentarily will be accompanied by an increased restriction to air flow in the space bounded by the lower side of the piston and the bridge, and this will be accompanied by a corresponding increase in the depression between the piston and throttle, which is immediately communicated to the interior of the suction chamber, instantly counteracting the initial disturbance by raising the piston to an appropriate extent.

The float chamber is of orthodox construction, comprising a needle valve (9) located within a separate seating which, in turn, is screwed in the float chamber lid, and a float (10), the upward movement of which, in response to the rising fuel level, causes final closure of the needle upon its seating through the medium of the hinged fork (11).

The float-chamber is a unit separate from the main body of the carburetor to which it is attached by means of the bolt (12), suitable drillings being provided therein to lead the fuel from the lower part of the float chamber to the region surrounding the jet. It is steadied at its upper extremity by a suction chamber attachment screw.

The buoyancy of the float, in conjunction with the form of the lever (11) is such that a fuel level is maintained approximately $1/8''$ below the jet bridge. This can easily be observed after first detaching the suction chamber and suction piston, and then lowering the jet to its full rich position. The level can vary a further $1/4''$ downwards without any ill effects on the functioning of the carburetor. The only parts of importance not so far described are those associated with the jet.

Under idling conditions the piston is completely dropped, being then supported by the two small protuberances provided on its lower surface, which are in contact with the bridge (28); the small gap thus formed between piston and bridge permits the flow of sufficient air to meet the idling demand of the engine without, however, creating enough depression on the induction side to raise the piston.

The fuel discharge required from the jet is very small under these conditions, hence the diameter of the portion of the needle now obstructing the mouth of the jet is very nearly equal to the jet bore. Initial manufacture of the complete carburetor assembly to the required degree of accuracy to ensure perfect concentricity between the needle and the jet bore under these conditions is impracticable, and an individual adjustment for this essential centralization is provided.

It will be seen that the jet is not mounted directly in the main body, but is housed in the parts (13) and (14) referred to as the jet bushes, or jet bearings.

The upper jet bush is provided with a flange which forms a face seal against a recess in the body, while the lower one carries a similar flange contacting the upper surface of the hollow hexagon locking nut (15).

The arrangement is such that tightening of the hollow hexagon locking screw will positively lock the jet and jet bushes in position. Some degree of lateral clearance is provided between the jet bushes and the bores formed in the main body and the locking screw. In this manner the assembly can be moved laterally until perfect concentricity of the jet and needle is achieved, the screw (15) being slackened for this purpose. This operation is referred to as centering the jet," on completion the jet locking nut (15) is finally tightened.

In addition to this concentricity adjustment, an axial adjustment of the jet is provided for the purpose of regulating the idling mixture strength.

Since, the needle tapers throughout its length, it will be clear that raising or lowering the jet within its bearing will alter the effective aperture of the jet orifice, and hence the rate of fuel discharge. To permit this adjustment the jet is a variably mounted within its bearings and provided with adequate sealing glands.

A compression spring (16) which, at its upper end, serves to compress the small sealing gland (17) and thus prevents any fuel leakage between the jet and the upper jet bearing.

At its lower end this spring abuts against a similar sealing gland, thus preventing leakage of fuel between the jet and the lower jet bearing.

In both locations a brass washer is interposed between the end of the spring and the sealing gland to take the spring thrust. A further sealing gland (19), together with a conical brass washer (20) is provided, to prevent fuel leakage between the jet screw (15) and the main body.

It will be seen from the diagram that the upward movement of the jet is determined by the position of the jet adjusting nut (18) since the enlarged jet head (21) finally abuts against this nut as the jet is moved upwards towards the "weak" or running position.

The position of the nut (18) therefore determines the idling mixture ratio setting of the carburetor for normal running with the engine hot, and is prevented from unintentional rotation by means of the loading spring (22).

The cold running mixture control mechanism comprises the jet lever (23) supported from the main body by the link member (24) and attached by means of a clevis pin to the jet head (21). A tension spring (25) is provided, as shown, to assist in returning the jet-moving mechanism to its normal running position. Connection is made from the outer extremity of the jet lever (23) to a control situated within reach of the driver.

Drillings in the float-chamber attachment bolt (12), the main body of the carburetor, the jet (5) and slots in the upper jet bearing (13) serve to conduct the fuel from the float-chamber to the jet orifice.

It will be seen that the spindle upon which the piston (3) is mounted is hollow, and that it surrounds a small stationary damper piston suspended from the suction chamber cap by means of the rod (26). The hollow interior of the spindle contains a quantity of thin engine oil, and the marked retarding effect upon the movement of the main piston assembly, occasioned by the resistance of the small piston, provides the momentary enrichment desirable when the throttle is abruptly opened. The damper piston is constructed to provide a one-way valve action which gives little resistance to the passage of the oil during the downward movement of the main piston.

An ignition connecting is provided for use in conjunction with vacuum-operated ignition advance mechanism, and is fitted to the front carburetor only.

Throttle and Mixture Control Interconnection

A direct connection is provided between the jet movement and the throttle opening. Such an interconnection ensures that

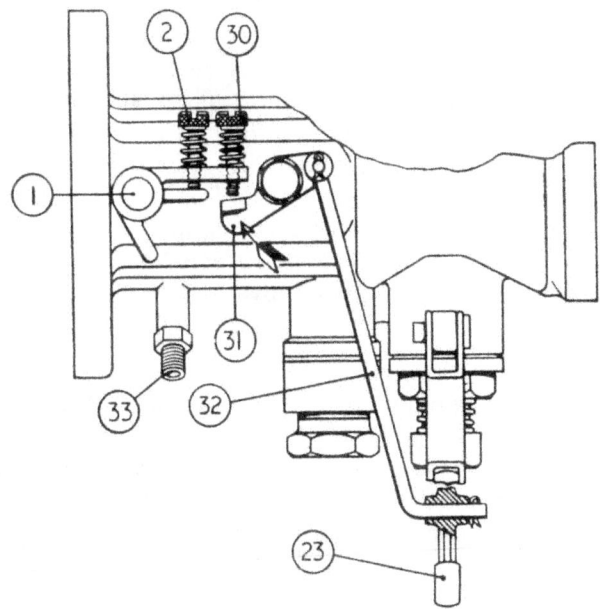

the engine will continue to run when the mixture is enriched by lowering the jet, without the additional necessity of maintaining a greater throttle opening than is normally provided by the setting of the slow-running screw (2).

The mechanism involved in this interconnection is shown above. It will be seen that a connecting rod (32) conveys movement from the jet lever (23) to a lever (31) pivoted on the side of the main body casting.

Movement of the jet lever in the direction of enrichment is thus accompanied by an upward movement of the extremity of the lever (31) which, in turn, abuts against the adjustable screw (30) and this opens the throttle to a greater degree than the normal slow-running setting controlled by the slow-running stop screw (2). The screw (30) should be so adjusted that it is just out of contact with the lever (31) when the jet has been raised to its normal running position, and the throttle is shut back to its normal idling condition, as determined by the screw (2).

Effect of Altitude and Climatic Extremes On Standard Tuning

The standard tuning employs a jet needle which is broadly suitable for temperate climates at sea level upwards to approximately 3,000 ft. Above this altitude it may be necessary, depending on the additional factors of extreme climatic heat and humidity, to use a weaker tuning than standard.

The factors of altitude, extreme climatic heat, each tend to demand a weaker tuning, and a combination of any of these factors would naturally emphasize this demand. This is a situation which cannot be met by a hard and fast factory recommendation owing to the wide variations in the condition existing and in such cases the owner will need to experiment with alternative weaker needles until one is found to be satisfactory.

If the carburetor is fitted with a spring-loaded suction piston, the necessary weakening may be affected by changing to a weaker type of spring or by its removal.

To Remove Jet Needle
1. Remove the air-cleaner.
2. Remove the damping piston from the top of the suction chamber.
3. Withdraw the three suction chamber securing screws and move the carburetor float chamber support arm to one side.
4. Lift the suction chamber and remove coil spring and washer from piston head.
5. Remove the piston with jet needle attached from the body

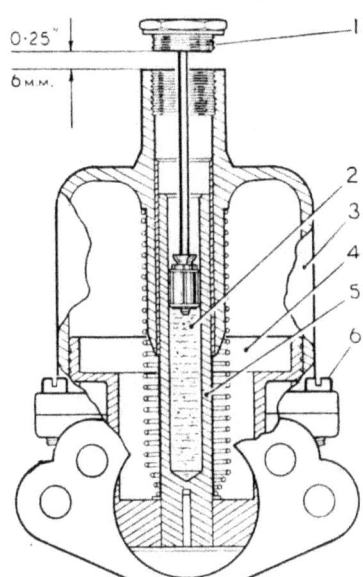

1 Damper
2 Oil well
3 Suction chamber
4 Piston
5 Piston rod
6 Screw

of the carburetor and empty away oil in the reservoir.
6. Loosen screw in base of piston and withdraw jet needle.

To Fit Needle
1. Ensure that the jet head is loose in the main body of the carburetor by loosening clamp ring.
2. Ascertain that the jet needle is perfectly straight and position it so that the shoulder is flush with the base of the piston, tighten screw to grip needle. Feed the needle into its recess in the jet head.
NOTE: On no account should the piston with the needle attached be laid down so that it rests on the needle. Failure to observe this point may cause carburetion defects due to a bent needle.
3. Position the washer and the spring on top of the piston and the suction chamber over the piston.
4. Secure with the three attachment screws with the foremost accommodating the float chamber support arm.
5. Fill the piston reservoir within thin oil and fit the damper to the suction chamber.
6. Centralize the jet as described below.

Centralization of Jet
1. Disconnect the throttle linkage to gain access to the jet head (21) and remove damper (26).

2. Withdraw the jet head (21) and remove adjusting nut (18) and spring (22). Replace nut (18) and screw up to its fullest extent.
3. Slide the jet head (21) into position until its head rests against the base of the adjusting nut.
4. The jet locking nut (15) should be slackened to allow the jet head (21) and bearings (13 and 14) assembly to move laterally.
5. The piston (3) should be raised, (access being gained through the air intake) and allowed to fall under its own weight. This should be repeated once or twice and the jet locking nut (15) tightened.
6. Check the piston by lifting to ascertain that there is complete freedom of movement. "If sticking is detected operation (4) and (5) will have to be repeated.
7. Withdraw jet head (21) and adjusting nut (18).
8. Replace nut (18) with spring (22) and insert the jet head (21).
9. Check oil reservoir and replace damper (26).
10. Tune the carburetors.

To Assemble the Carburetor

Having ensured the cleanliness and the serviceability of all component parts, it is suggested that the carburetor be assembled in the following sequence:

The front carburetor differs from that of the rear insomuch that there are certain additions. As and when the additions occur they will be specifically mentioned.)
1. Fit the ignition union to the front carburetor, this utilizes the tapped bore which breaks through into the mixture passage.
2. Position the throttle spindle in the body in such a manner that the spindle protrudes **less** on the left-hand side looking at the air cleaner ends.
3. Feed the throttle disc into the slot of the spindle and secure with two countersunk screws. These screws have split shanks which are now opened by the insertion of the screw driver blade.
4. Position the throttle stop with the two adjusting screws on the shorter end of the throttle spindle of the front carburetor body and secure with the taper pin; to the rear carburetor, fit the throttle stop with the single adjusting screw.
5. Feed the rocker lever bolt through the double coil washer and the rocker lever so that the platform of the lever is on the left viewing the bolt head. This assembly is fitted to the front carburetor with a plain washer between it and the carburetor. Ensure that the rocker lever moves freely.

6. Fit the throttle spindle return spring anchor plate on the longer end of the spindle and anchor it on the web provided. Follow it with the spring and the end clip then adjust the tension and lock the end clip with the pinch bolt.
7. To the bottom half of the jet bearing position the copper washer followed by the jet adjusting sealing nut (threaded portion uppermost) spring and secure with the jet adjusting nut. Position the alloy sealing ring, flatter side downwards, and the cork washer over the thread of the jet adjusting nut.
8. Insert the jet assembly through the jet adjusting nut and bottom half of the jet bearing from below. Position the cork gland washer, the copper gland washer, spring, a second gland washer and cork gland washer on the head of the jet assembly.
9. Position a copper washer on the shoulders of the upper half jet bearing and, with the shoulder uppermost, balance the top half bearing on the cork gland washer of the jet assembly.
10. Feed the assembly mentioned in (6) and (9) into the carburetor body and secure with the sealing nut.
11. Fit the float to the pillar of the float chamber, this is symmetrical and can be fitted either way up.
12. The needle valve body is secured in the float chamber cover, position valve needle and hinge lever and insert pin.
13. Assemble the splash overflow pipe to the cap of float chamber with a washer interposed between.
14. Fit the float chamber cover to the float chamber and attach cap nut. The nut is left loose at this juncture.
15. Fit the jet needle to the piston assembly and ensure that its lower shoulder is flush with that of the piston.
16. The piston and jet needle is now fitted to the body assembly so that the brass dowel in the carburetor body locates the longitudinal groove in the piston.
17. With the smaller diameter of the coil spring downwards, position the spring over the polished stem of the piston.
18. Fit the suction chamber over the spring and piston stem allowing the spring to position itself outside the suction chamber center.
19. The suction chamber is secured to the carburetor body by three screws, these are fitted but left loose at this juncture.
20. The float chamber is now attached to the carburetor body by the float chamber attachment bolt. Two large bore fiber washers with a brass washer between are positioned between the bolt head and the float chamber and a small bore washer between the float chamber and the body. With the washers so

placed the float chamber is attached to the body, the attachment bolt is left loose at this juncture.

21. Looking at the intake end of the carburetor body remove the right-hand suction chamber securing screw. With a shakeproof washer under its head feed the bolt through the float chamber steady bracket and replace to secure suction chamber. The three screws can now be fully tightened, the cap nut is, however, still left loose. The cap nut of the cover is tightened to secure the splash overflow pipe for tuning purposes when fitted to the car. Attach the jet lever return spring to the position provided between jet assembly and float chamber.

22. The jet and jet needle are now centralized.

23. The damper assembly is fitted to the suction chamber dry. The oil reservoir is not filled until the carburetors are fitted to the car.

24. Select the jet lever of the front carburetor, identified by having two holes at the extremity of the longer arm. This is attached to the jet assembly by a clevis pin and split pin, positioning the second end of the lever return spring to the jet lever.

25. Feed the upper end of the tension link through the rocker lever of the front carburetor from behind and the second end through the jet lever. Secure both ends with split pins.

26. Select the front carburetor jet lever link, this is distinguished by the pinch bolt at one end. This is attached to the lug at the rear of the jet assembly and again to the elbow of the jet lever in such a manner that the pinch bolt end of this link points to the rear. Both attachments are made by clevis pins and split pins.

The assembly of the jet lever and jet lever link to the rear carburetor is very similar. Both components are shorter than those fitted to the front carburetor.

To Adjust the Fuel Level in the Float Chamber

The level of the fuel in the float chamber is adjusted by setting the fork lever in the float chamber lid. It is suggested that the following procedure for its adjustment is adopted.

1. Remove the banjo bolt of the fuel connection and collect the two fiber washers and filter.
2. Loosen the screw securing the float chamber support arm to the carburetor body.
3. Withdraw the cap nut from the center of the float chamber lid and remove washers and splash overflow pipe.
4. Swing the support arm clear to lift the lid of the float chamber and joint washer.

The piston (3) is designed to lift the jet needle (6) by the depression transferred to the top side from the passage facing the butterfly. This depression overcomes the weight of the piston and spring (8). The piston should move freely over its entire range and rest on the bridge pieces (28) when the engine is not running.

This should be checked by gently lifting the piston with a small screwdriver and any tendency for binding generally indicates one of the following faults:—

a. The damper rod may be bent causing binding and this can be checked by its removal. If the piston is now free the damper rod should be straightened and refitted.

b. The piston is meant to be a fine clearance fit at its outer diameter in the suction chamber and a sliding fit in the central bush. The suction chamber should be removed, complete with piston, and the freedom of movement checked after removal of the damper rod. The assembly should be washed clean and very lightly oiled where this slides in the bush and then checked for any tendency of binding. It is permissible to carefully remove, with a hand scaper, any high spots on the outer wall of the suction chamber, but no attempt should be made to increase the clearance by increasing the general bore of the suction chamber or decreasing the diameter of the piston. The fit of the piston in its central bush should be checked under both rotational and sliding movement.

Eccentricity of Jet and Needle.

The jet (14) is a loose fit in its recess and must always be centered by the needle before locking up the clamping ring (15).

The needle should be checked in the piston to see that it is not bent. It will be realized that it does not matter if it is eccentric as the adjustment of the jet allows for this, but a bent needle can never have the correct adjustment.

Flooding from Float Chamber or Mouth of Jet

This can be caused by a punctured float (10) or dirt on the needle valve (9) or its seat. These latter items can be readily cleaned after removal of the float chamber lid.

Leakage from Bottom of Jet adjacent to Adjustment Nut

Leakage in this vicinity is most likely due to defective sealing by the upper and lower gland assemblies. There is no remedy other than removing the whole jet assembly after disconnecting the operating lever and cleaning or replacing the faulty parts. It is very important that all parts are replaced in their correct sequence, as shown in the illustration, and it must be realized that centralization of the jet and needle and re-tuning will be necessary after this operation.

Dirt in the Carburetor

This should be checked in the normal way by examining and cleaning the float chamber, but it may be necessary if excessive water or dirt is present to strip down and clean all parts of the carburetor with solvent.

Failure of Fuel Supply to Float Chamber

If the engine is found to stop under idling or light running conditions, notwithstanding the fact that a good supply of fuel is present at the float chamber inlet union (observable by momentarily disconnecting this), it is possible that the needle has become stuck to its seating. This possibility arises in the rare cases where some gummy substance is present in the fuel system. The most probable instance of this nature is the polymerized gum which sometimes results from the protracted storage of fuel in the tank. After removal of the float chamber lid and float lever, the needle may be withdrawn, and its point thoroughly cleaned by immersion in alcohol.

Similar treatment should also be applied to the needle seating, which can conveniently be cleaned by means of a matchstick dipped in alcohol. Persistent trouble of this nature can only be cured properly by complete mechanical cleansing of the tank and fuel system. If the engine is found to suffer from a serious lack of power which becomes evident at higher speeds and loads, this is probably due to an inadequately sustained fuel supply, and the fuel pump should be investigated for inadequate delivery, and any filters in the system inspected and cleansed.

Sticking Jet

Should the jet and its operating mechanism become unduly resistant to the action of lowering and raising by means of the enrichment mechanism, the jet should be lowered to its fullest extent, and the lower part thus exposed should be smeared with petroleum jelly, or similar lubricant. Oil should be applied to the various linkage pins in the mechanism and the jet raised and lowered several times in order to promote the passage of the lubricant upwards between the jet and its surrounding parts.

TUNING & SYNCHRONIZING S.U. CARBURETORS

The following procedure will cover the steps necessary to tune and synchronize a pair of S.U.s regardless of the type of engine involved.

Idling mixture and idling speed adjustments have an important effect on the performance of the automobile. Therefore the on-vehicle adjustments and synchronization of two or more carburetors tend to be somewhat critical. The normal procedure is explained below and can be followed through with a minimum of tools. However, the SU TOOL or UNISYN instrument mentioned later are advised.

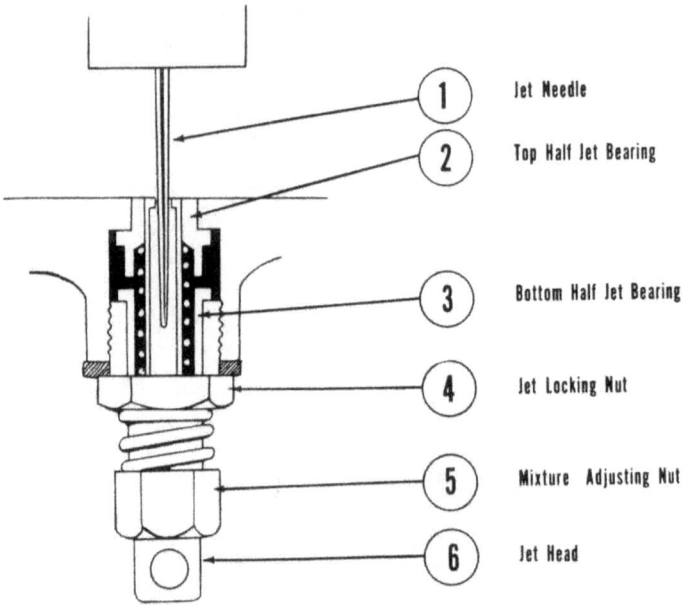

1. Jet Needle
2. Top Half Jet Bearing
3. Bottom Half Jet Bearing
4. Jet Locking Nut
5. Mixture Adjusting Nut
6. Jet Head

1. Remove the two air cleaners by removing the securing bolts that hold the air cleaners to the carburetor flange. Put aside for later servicing.
2. Disconnect the throttle linkage between the two carbs by loosening the nut on the folded clamp. See Figure 39. This permits individual adjustment of the carburetors to bring them into synchronization.
3. Disconnect the choke cable and the mixture control linkage between the carburetors, by removing the pin in the forked end of the jet control connecting rod.

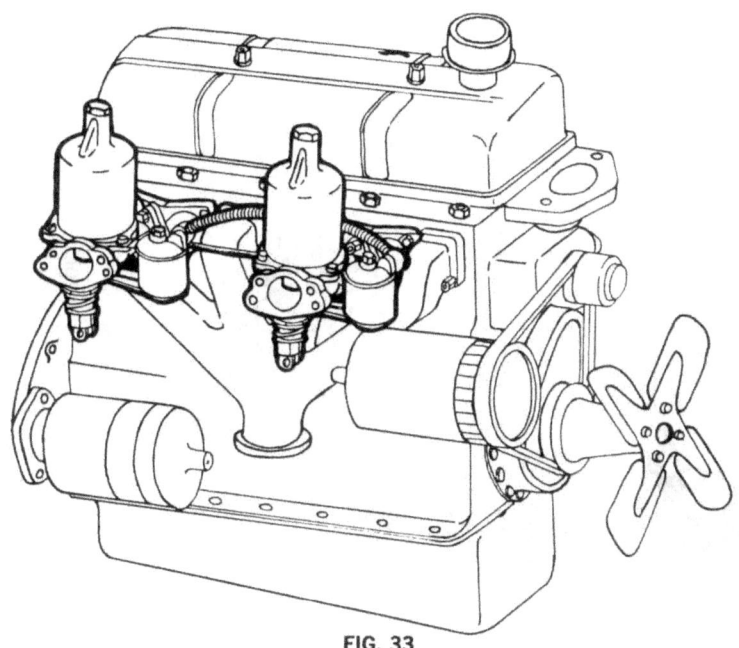

FIG. 33

4. Remove the damper piston by unscrewing the brass securing nut on top of the carburetor suction chamber.
5. Remove the suction chamber by removing the brass screws around the base. Move the arm that goes to the float bowl out of the way.
6. Remove the suction chamber and lift out the coil spring from the piston.

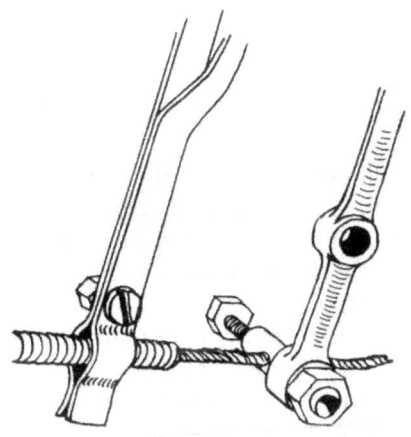

FIG. 34

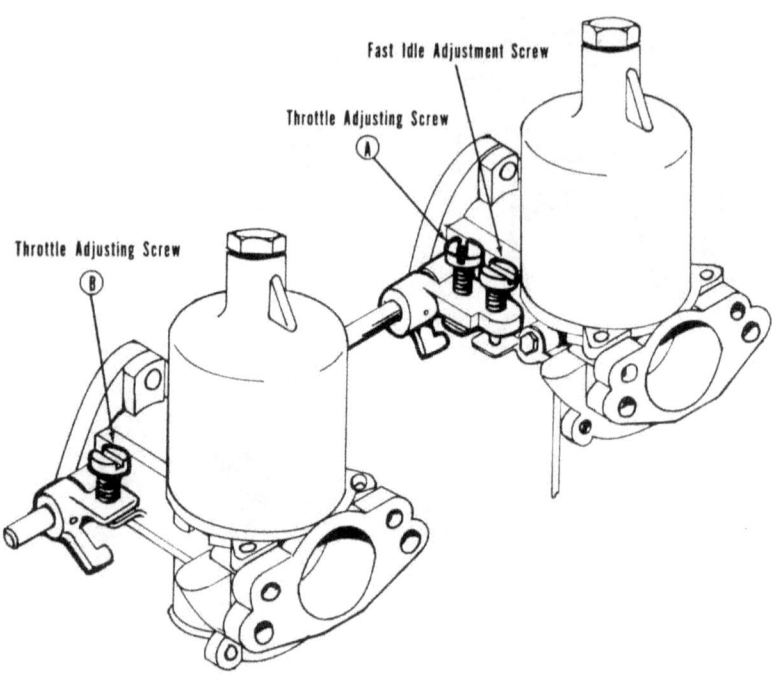

FIG. 36

7. Lift the piston straight up and pour out the oil in the reservoir. Check to see that the jet needle shoulder is flush with the bottom face of the piston. Examine the jet needle for wear that indicates the jet needle is not centered in the jet. Evidence of wear requires that the needle be replaced and checked for centering.

Regardless of the type of needle installed, it should set flush with the bottom face of the piston.

8. Slip the spring over the piston and slide the piston into position.
9. Replace the suction chamber, the support arm to the float bowl, and fasten in place with the brass screws.
10. Fill the hydraulic damper with oil and secure the damper piston washer and nut. Multi-grade (10-30) engine oil is excellent for this purpose.
11. Start the engine and allow it to warm up to operating temperature. Release the folded coupling on the throttle spindle connecting rod (Figure 39) preparatory to synchronization.
12. Adjust each throttle adjusting screw A and B in Figure 36 until the engine is turning over at approximately 500 rpm.

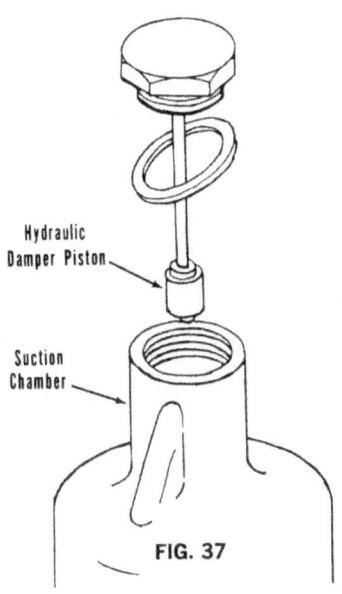

FIG. 37

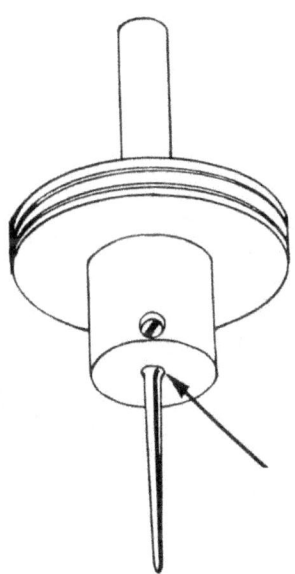

FIG. 38

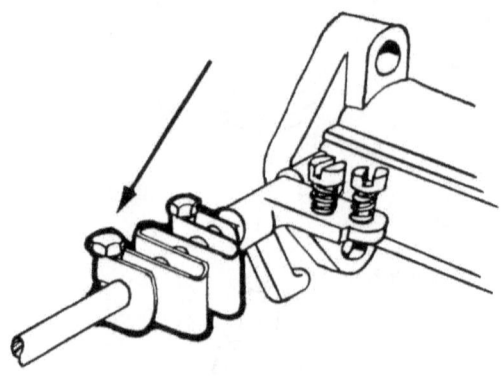

FIG. 39

13. **Adjusting by ear.** Listen to the hiss produced at each carburetor. If the intensity of the hiss is different, unscrew the throttle adjusting screw on the carburetor with the lower hiss and screw in on the adjusting screw of the other carburetor until the hiss from the two carburetors is the same. A short length of tubing can be used to isolate each carburetor — like a stethescope is used by a physician.

14. **Use of the UNI-SYN.** The UNI-SYN permits a much more accurate adjustment of the carburetor synchronization than is possible with the ears alone. The UNI-SYN is used in the following way:

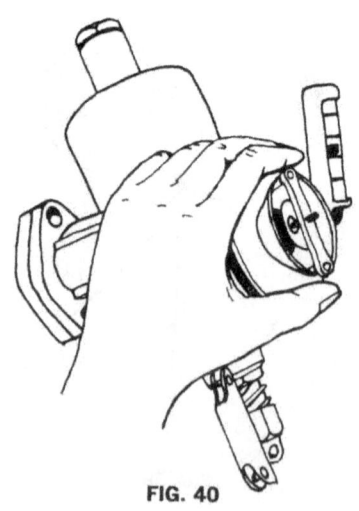

FIG. 40

a. Place the UNI-SYN over the throat of the right hand carburetor.

b. Adjust orofice screw on the UNI-SYN until the float rises to a graduation mark near the middle of the tube. Actually any of the marks may be used as a reference.

c. Place the UNI-SYN on the left hand carburetor.

d. Adjust the throttle adjusting screw on the left hand carburetor until the float·rises to the same graduation as before in step (b).

e. Place the UNI-SYN over each carburetor throat in turn and re-check, noting the float level, and trim the throttle adjusting screws until the float rises to the same level for both carbs. When the indication is the same for the two carbs, the throttles are in sync. If idle speed has increased, it is only necessary to back off on the throttle screws an equal amount.

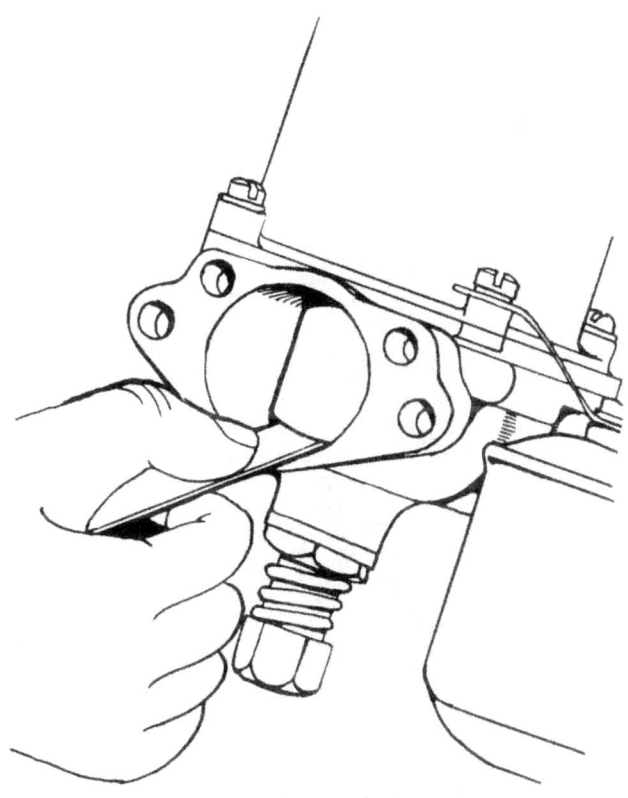

FIG. 41

15. **Mixture Adjustment.** Screw the adjusting nuts C in Figure 42 as far as they will go in a clockwise direction, looking from the bottom of the carburetor. Then back off the adjusting nuts about two and a half turns or about 16 flats of the adjusting nut. This serves as a starting point.

16. Using a small screw driver or a small piece of aluminum filed to the proper shape, lift the piston of each carburetor in turn no more than $\frac{1}{32}$ inch and carefully note if the engine speeds up or slows down.

a. Engine speeds up — Screw in on the adjusting screw until no engine rpm change is noticed when the piston is lifted.

b. Engine slows down — Back off on the adjusting nut a flat at a time until no change in engine speed occurs when the piston is lifted.

The fuel air mixture adjustment is correct when lifting of the piston causes no change in engine speed.

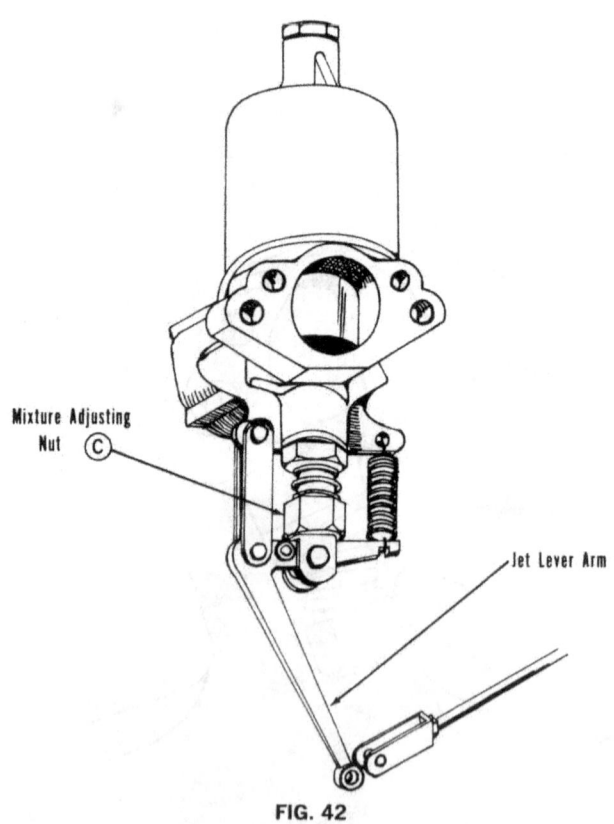

FIG. 42

17. **Check for Piston Hangup.** When you are satisfied that you have the mixture adjusted correctly, check the piston in each carburetor to see that it is free to move its full range without sticking or hanging up against the walls of the suction chamber. Do this by carefully lifting the piston about $1/2$ inch, letting it fall and noting if it returns to the idle position smoothly. If there is any tendency to stick or hang up, check the following:
a. Check the hydraulic damper rod for a bend.
b. Check for rubbing of the piston against the suction chamber.
c. Check to see that the jet needle is not rubbing against the jet.

The SU Tool

One of the best, least expensive non-mechanical aids to the performance of the carburetor tuning process is the "SU Tool" (in reality a kit of tools) which greatly speeds up the functions of checking piston free movement, synchronization of two or three carburetors, testing mixture strength, adjusting float level and centering the jet needle. The SU Tool is distributed by Messrs. MG Mitten Co., 1163 E. Green St., Pasadena, California, USA and inquiries should be directed to that firm relative to purchase.

In principle, the SU Tool achieves synchronization at any rpm from idling to top speed without the necessity for removing air cleaners by making it possible to visually check the height of the pistons in two or more carburetors simultaneously. The test rods of the tool kit allow the pistons to be lifted and dropped accurately to check free movement or mixture strength. The rods are also precision made for use as gauges for float level setting. A jet pin, which is used to replace the needle permits accurate centering without danger of bending the needle itself. The jet wrench included in the kit is made specifically for the jet adjusting nut and is conveniently short for easy manipulation.

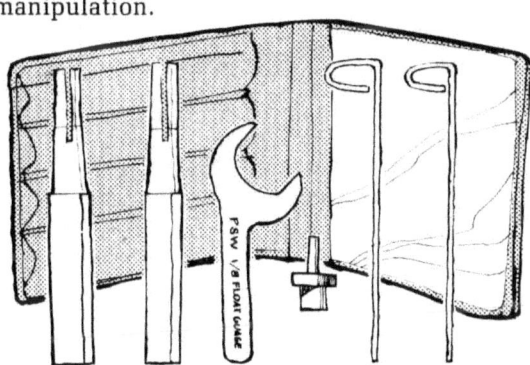

NOTES

AUSTIN HEALEY

Since 1953 when the first Austin Healey 100 was introduced, the carburetors have been basically the same. All models are S.U. carburetors with variations in choke diameter and configuration. Here are the standard carburetors and jet needles.

Model	Carburetor	Needle
100	H-4 (pair)	QW
Le Mans	H-6 (pair)	OA7
100S	H-6 (pair)	KWI
BN-4 (3-port)	H-4 (pair)	AJ
BN-6, BN-7	HD-6 (pair)	CV
BN7 (1961)	HD-6 (pair)	DJ
3000 Mk II	HS-4 (three)	DJ
3000 Mk II	HS-6 (pair)	BC

Certain cars, beginning with engine 29D/U/H2864, have been fitted with the HD-6 Thermo-carburetor having a thermostatically controlled auxiliary carburetor for cold starting in place of the manually-operated choke. A discussion of it follows the sections on H and HD types.

THE H TYPE CARBURETORS

The two S.U. carburetors are of the variable jet type, fitted with air cleaners.

A damper is provided in each carburetor, consisting of a plunger and non-return valve attached to the oil cap nut, and operates in the hollow piston rod which is partly filled with oil. Its suction is to give a slightly enriched mixture on acceleration by controlling the rise of the piston and to prevent piston flutter.

MAINTENANCE

Remove the suction chamber cap and damper assembly and replenish the oil reservoir as necessary every 1,000 miles (1600 km.). It is first essential to run the engine until it has attained its normal running temperature before commencing any mixture or slow-running adjustments

The slow-running is governed by the setting of the jet adjusting screws and the throttle stop screws, all of which must be correctly set and synchronized if satisfactory results are to be obtained.

The two throttles are interconnected by a coupling shaft and spring coupling clips which enable them to be correctly synchronized when adjustments take place.

Before blaming the carburetor settings for bad slow-running, make sure that it is not due to badly set contact points, faulty plugs, bad valve clearance setting or faulty valves and valve springs.

Good slow-running cannot be obtained if the setting for the jets is incorrect. It is therefore advisable to commence any adjustments at this point.

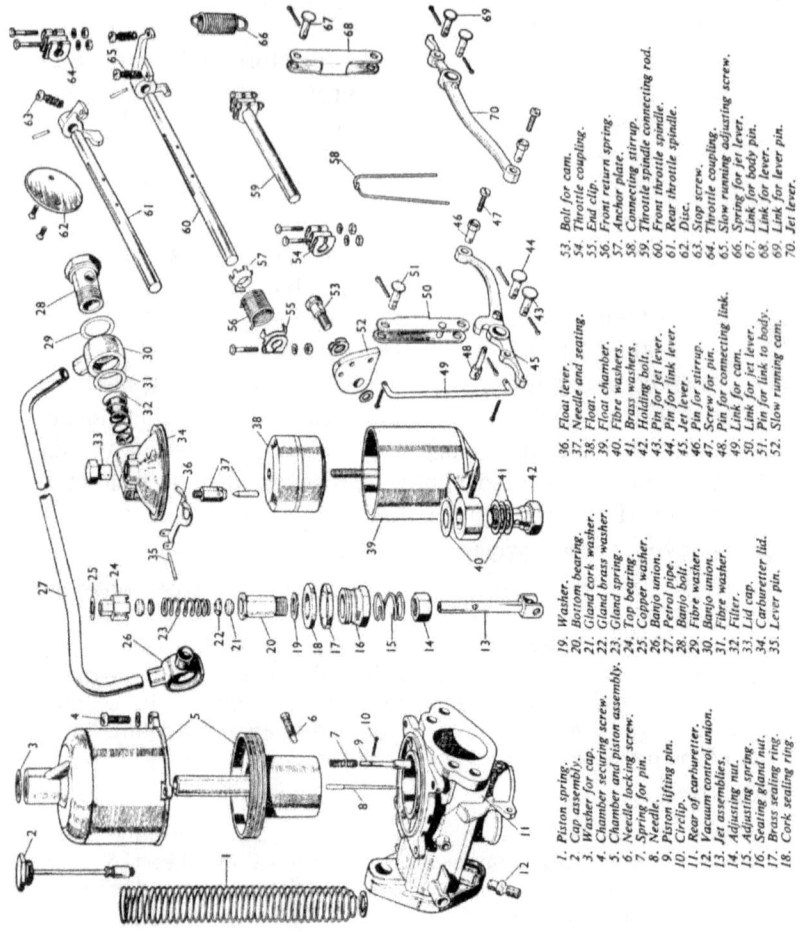

1. Piston spring.
2. Cap assembly.
3. Washer for cap.
4. Chamber securing screw.
5. Chamber and piston assembly.
6. Needle locking screw.
7. Spring for pin.
8. Needle.
9. Piston lifting pin.
10. Circlip.
11. Rear of carburetter.
12. Vacuum control union.
13. Jet assemblies.
14. Adjusting nut.
15. Adjusting spring.
16. Sealing gland nut.
17. Brass sealing ring.
18. Cork sealing ring.
19. Washer.
20. Bottom bearing.
21. Gland cork washer.
22. Gland brass washer.
23. Gland spring.
24. Top bearing.
25. Copper washer.
26. Banjo union.
27. Petrol pipe.
28. Banjo bolt.
29. Fibre washer.
30. Banjo union.
31. Fibre washer.
32. Filter.
33. Lid cap.
34. Carburetter lid.
35. Lever pin.
36. Float lever.
37. Needle and seating.
38. Float.
39. Float chamber.
40. Fibre washers.
41. Brass washers.
42. Holding bolt.
43. Pin for jet lever.
44. Pin for link lever.
45. Jet lever.
46. Pin for stirrup.
47. Screw for pin.
48. Pin for connecting link.
49. Link for cam.
50. Link for jet lever.
51. Pin for link to body.
52. Slow running cam.
53. Bolt for cam.
54. Throttle coupling.
55. End clip.
56. Front return spring.
57. Anchor plate.
58. Connecting stirrup.
59. Throttle spindle connecting rod.
60. Front throttle spindle.
61. Rear throttle spindle.
62. Disc.
63. Stop screw.
64. Throttle coupling.
65. Slow running adjusting screw.
66. Spring for jet lever.
67. Link for body pin.
68. Link for lever.
69. Link for lever pin.
70. Jet lever.

As noted in the index, certain of the carburetor models discussed here are also fitted to other automobile makes. Some minor differences in mounting and linkage prevail, but all maintenance and adjustment data given here can be applied.

In order to adjust the carburetors successfully it is necessary to remove the air cleaners and intake pipe assembly from the carburetors and engine valve cover and make sure the pistons work freely and the jets are properly centered unless the S.U. Tool mentioned earlier is used. If it is not available, follow this procedure:

Adjusting the Jets

1 — Slacken off the pinch-bolt of one of the spring coupling clips locating the inter-connecting shaft to the carbuletor throttle spindles and also release the two screws securing the choke spring to the jet levers, so that each carburetor can be operated independently.

2 — Release the throttle lever adjusting screws until both throttles are completely closed.

3 — Turn the throttle lever adjusting screw for the rear carburetor clockwise until it is just touching the web on the carburetor body and then give it one full turn. This will set the rear carburetor for fast idling and leave the front one out of action. This can be ensured further by lifting the front carburetor piston a matter of ½ in. (13 mm.).

4 — With the engine running, set the jet adjusting screw for the rear carburetor so that a mixture strength is obtained which will give the best running speed for this throttle opening, taking care to see that the jet head is kept in firm contact with the adjusting nut the whole time.

5 — The correctness or otherwise of this setting can be checked by raising the suction piston with a small screwdriver, or similar instrument, to the extent of 1/32 in. (1 mm.). This should cause a very slight momentary increase in the engine speed without impairing the evenness of the running in any way.

If this operation has the effect of stopping the engine it is an indication that the mixture setting is too weak.

If an appreciable speed increase occurs and continues to occur when the piston is raised as much as ¼ in. (16 mm.) it is an indication that the mixture is too rich.

6 — When the rear carburetor mixture setting has been carried out correctly release its throttle adjusting screw so that it is clear of the stop and the throttle completely closed, and lift the piston ½ in. (13 mm.) to render it inoperative. Then repeat the jet-adjusting operation on the front carburetor.

7 — When both carburetors are correctly adjusted individually for mixture strength the throttles of each should be set so as to give the required slow-running and synchronization.

Slow-running and Synchronization

Screw each throttle lever adjusting screw so that its end is only just making contact with the web on the carburetor body, then give each screw one full turn exactly.

Start the engine, which will now idle on the fast side.

Unscrew each throttle lever adjusting screw an equal amount, a fraction of a turn at a time, until the desired slow-running speed is achieved.

Correct synchronization can be checked by listening at each carburetor air intake through a length of rubber tube and noticing if the noise produced by the incoming air is the same at both. Any variation in the intensity of the sound indicates that one throttle is set more widely open than the other—the louder sound indicating the throttle with the greater opening.

When the same intensity of sound is given by both carburetors the intercoupling shaft clip should be tightened up firmly to ensure that the throttles work in unison.

If a Unisyn is available it should be used to give a visual indication of incoming air.

Since the delivery characteristics, when both carburetors are operating together, vary somewhat from those existing when each is working separately, it will be found necessary to check them again for correctness of mixture strength by lifting the pistons in turn as described in **"Adjusting the Jets,"** making such adjustments of the jet adjusting screws as are required to balance the mixture.

Fitting New Needles

If the road performance is not satisfactory after the above adjustments have been made, larger or smaller needles may be necessary. To change the needles, remove the screws and lift off the suction chambers, having marked them to ensure their refitting to their respective carburetors. Remove the pistons and return springs.

Unscrew the screw at the side of each piston tube and withdraw the needles.

Fit the new needles: a needle should be fitted with its shoulder flush with the face of the piston as shown in the drawing.

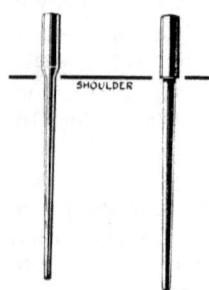

The Float-chamber

The position of the forked lever in the float-chamber must be such that the level of the float (and therfore the height of the fuel at the jet) is correct.

This is checked by inserting a 7/16 in. (11.11 mm.) round bar between the forked lever and the machined lip of the float-chamber lid. The prongs of the lever should just rest on the bar when the needle is on its setting. If this is not so, the lever should be reset at the point where the prongs meet the shank. Care must be taken not to bend the shank, which must be perfectly flat and at right angles to the needle when it is on its seating.

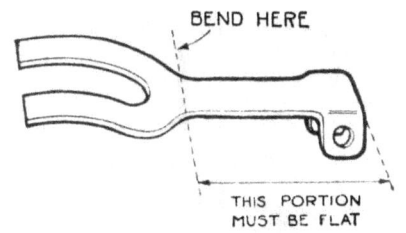

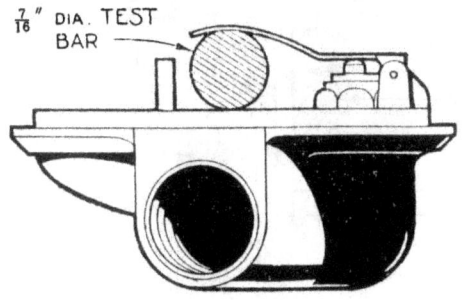

The correct setting of the float lever.

Centering a Jet

First remove the clevis pin at the bose of the jet which attaches the jet head to the jet operating lever; withdraw the jet completely, and remove the adjusting nut and the adjusting nut spring. Replace the adjusting nut without its spring and screw it up to the highest position. Slide the jet into position until the jet head is against the base of the adjusting nut. When this has been done, feel if the piston is perfectly free by lifting it up with the finger with the dashpot piston removed. If it is not, slacken the jet holding screw and manipulate the lower part of the assembly, including the projecting part of the bottom half jet bearing, adjusting nut and jet head. Make sure that this assembly is now slightly loose. The piston should then rise and fall quite freely as the needle is now able to move the jet into the required central position. The jet holding screw should now be tightened and a check made to determine that the piston is still quite free. If it is not found to be so, the jet holding screw should be slackened again and the operation repeated. When complete freedom of the piston is achieved the jet adjusting nut should be removed, together with the jet, and the spring replaced. The adjusting nut should now be screwed back to its original position.

Experience shows that a large percentage of carburetors have had jets removed and incorrectly centered on replacement.

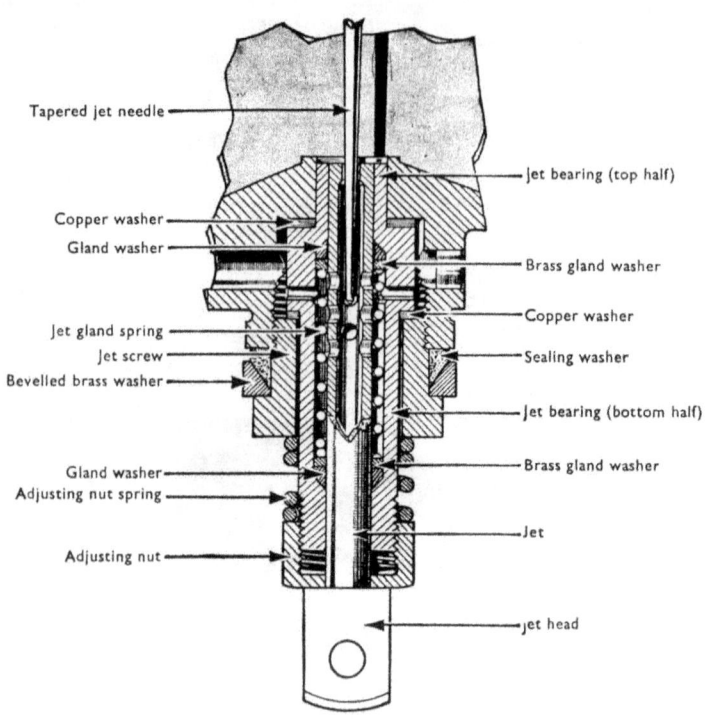

The jet assembly.

SOURCES OF CARBURETOR TROUBLE
Piston Sticking
The piston assembly comprises the suction disc and the piston forming the choke, into which is inserted the hardened and ground piston rod which engages in a bearing in the center of the suction chamber and in which is, in turn, inserted the jet needle. The piston rod running in the bearing is the only part which is in actual contact with any other part, the suction disc, piston, and needle all having suitable clearances to prevent sticking. If sticking does occur the whole assembly should be cleaned carefully and the piston rod lubricated with a spot of thin oil. No oil must be applied to any other part except the piston rod. A sticking piston can be ascertained by removing the dashpot piston damper, inserting a finger in the air intake and lifting the piston, which should come up quite freely and fall back smartly onto its seating when released.

Water or dirt in the Carburetor
When this is suspected, lift the piston: the jet can then be seen. Flood the carburetor and watch the jet; if the fuel does not flow through freely there is a blockage. To remedy this, start the engine, open the throttle, and block up the air inlet momentarily without shutting the throttle, keeping the throttle open until the engine

starts to race. This trouble seldom arises with the S.U. carburetor owing to the size of the jet and fuel ways. When it does happen the above method will nearly always clear it. Should it not do so, the only alternative is to remove the jet.

Float-chamber Flooding

This can be seen by the fuel flowing over the float-chamber and dripping from the air inlet, and is generally caused by grit between the float-chamber needle and its guide. This can usually be cured by depressing the float depressing plunger to allow the incoming flow of fuel to wash the grit through the guide and into the float-chamber.

Float Needle Sticking

If the engine stops, apparently through lack of fuel, when there is plenty in the tank and the pump is working properly, the probable cause is a sticking float needle. An easy test for this is to disconnect the pipe from the electric pump to the carburetor, switch on the ignition to heck if fuel is delivered; if it is, starvation has almost certainly been caused by the float needle sticking to its seating, and the float-chamber lid should therefore be removed, the needle and seating cleaned, and refitted. At the same time it will be advisable to clean out the entire fuel feed system, as this trouble is caused by foreign matter in the fuel, and unless this is removed it is likely to recur. It is of no use whatever renewing any of the component parts of the carburetor, and the only cure is to make sure that the fuel tank and pipe lines are entirely free from any kind of foreign matter or sticky substance capable of causing this trouble.

THE AIR CLEANERS

Remove the units and wash the gauze in gasoline every 6,000 miles (9600 km.) or every 3,000 miles (4800 km.) in exceptionallly dusty conditions. When the gauze is clean and dry, re-oil it with engine oil

THE H.D. TYPE CARBURETORS

The S.U. H.D. carburetors are fitted to 6 port cylinder head engines. They differ from the more familiar S.U. type in so far that the jet glands are replaced by a flexible diaphragm, and the idling mixture is conducted along a passage-way, in which is located a metering screw, instead of being controlled by the throttle disc; the throttle and jet interconnection mechanism is also re-designed.

The jet (1) which is fed through its lower end is attached to a synthetic rubber diaphragm (5) by means of the jet cup (4) and jet return spring cup (7), the center of the diaphragm being depressed between these two parts; at its outer edge it is held between the diaphragm casing (9) and the float-chamber arm. The jet (1) is controlled by the jet return spring (8) and the jet actuating lever (10), the latter having an adjusting screw (18) which limits the upward travel of the jet (1) and thus constitutes the idler adjustment; screwing it in (clockwise) enriches the mixture, and unscrewing it weakens the mixture.

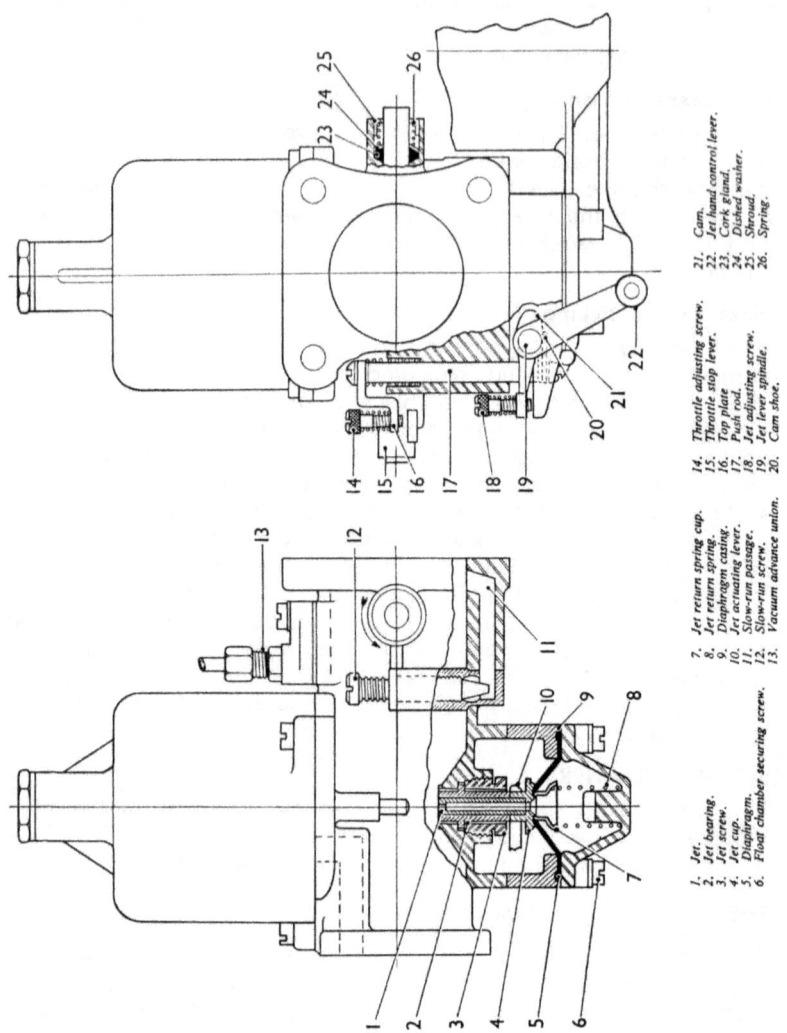

1. Jet.
2. Jet bearing.
3. Jet screw.
4. Jet cup.
5. Diaphragm.
6. Float chamber securing screw.
7. Jet return spring cup.
8. Jet return spring.
9. Diaphragm casing.
10. Jet actuating lever.
11. Slow-run passage.
12. Slow-run screw.
13. Vacuum advance union.
14. Throttle adjusting screw.
15. Throttle stop lever.
16. Top plate
17. Push rod.
18. Jet adjusting screw.
19. Jet lever spindle.
20. Cam shoe.
21. Cam.
22. Jet hand control lever.
23. Cork gland.
24. Dished washer.
25. Shroud.
26. Spring.

Throttle and Jet Interconnection

The throttle and jet interconnection mechanism is operated by a cam (21) mounted on the jet lever spindle (19), the whole being housed in the diaphragm casing (9). The cam (2) on being rotated by means of the jet hand control lever (22) actuates the cam shoe (20), thereby causing vertical movement of the push-rod (17). To the top of this push-rod is attached the top plate (16), which is fitted with an adjusting screw making contact with the throttle stop lever (15).

It will be seen that angular movement of the jet hand control lever (22) will turn the jet lever spindle (19) and, therefore, the jet actuating lever (10) controls the jet cup (4) and the jet (1). The cam controls the cam shoe (20), push-rod (17), top plate (16) and the throttle. Suitable setting of the two adjustments screws (14) and (18) will give any desired combination of mixture enrichment and throttle opening.

Vacuum Controlled Ignition and Economizer Ports

The connection to the vacuum ignition control is made at the top of the carburetor instead of underneath or at the side, as with the older type.

Throttle Spindle Glands

Provision is made for the use of throttle spindle glands consisting of the cork gland itself (23), a dished retaining washer (24), a spring (26) and a shroud (25). This assembly should not require servicing and can only be removed by dismantling the throttle spindle and disc.

Idling

The H.D. carburetor idles on the main jet, the mixture, passing under the throttle disc, is conducted along the passage-way (11) connecting the choke space to the other side of the throttle disc. The quantity of mixture passing through the passage-way (11) and, therefore, the idling speed of the engine, is controlled by the "slow-run" valve (12), the quality, or relative richness of the mixture, being determined by the jet adjusting screw (18). It follows that when idling, once the engine has reached its running temperature, the throttle remains completely closed against the bore of the carburetor; for fast idle, when the engine is cold, it continues to be partially open, the mixture passing under the throttle disc as well as along the passage-way (11).

Centering the Jet

This is carried out in much the same way as on the standard type carburetor, except that the float-chamber must be removed and the jet held in the uppermost position by hand, the jet adjusting screw (18) having first been undone sufficiently to allow the jet cup (4) to make contact with the jet bearing (2), with a distinct clearance between the jet adjusting screw (18) and its abutment. It is important to keep the diaphragm and therefore the jet in the same radial position, in relation to the carburetor body and jet casing throughout this operation, as the jet orifice is not necessarily concentric with its outside diameter, and turning might cause decentralization. The simplest way to do this is to mark one of the diaphragm and corresponding jet screw casing holes with a soft pencil.

Adjustment

The adjustment of the H.D. carburetor is extremely simple. Whereas with the older type the jet was controlled by a nut, it is now set by a screw (18), and whereas the engine speed was determined by adjustment of the throttle, it is now controlled by the "slow-run" valve (12). To enrich the mixture the screw (18) should be screwed in, and to increase the idling speed the "slow-run" valve (12) should be unscrewed.

The adjustment procedure is as follows:

1 — Run the engine until its normal operating temperature is reached.

2 — Disconnect the interconnecting rod between the jet actuating levers.

3 — The throttle stop screws on each carburetor must be undone so that they are clear of the stops. This ensures that the throttles are fully closed.

4 — Screw the slow running valve screw right down on each instrument and then unscrew them 2¼ turns.

5 — If the engine runs too fast when this has been done, screw in both slow running screws a little at a time until even idling is achieved.

6 — Set the mixture strength by means of the jet lever adjusting screws.

7 — The correctness of this setting can be checked by raising the suction piston with a small screwdriver, or the piston lifting pin, to the extent of 1/32 inch (1 mm.). This should cause a very slight momentary increase in the engine speed without impairing the evenness of the running in any way. If this operation has the effect of stapping the engine it is an indication that the mixture setting is too weak.

If an appreciable speed increase occurs and continues to occur when the piston is raised as much as ¼ inch (6 mm.) it is an indication that the mixture is too rich.

8 — The interconnecting rod should now be refitted taking care not to alter the positions of the jet actuating levers. It may be necessary to adjust its length.

9 — With the foregoing adjustments complete, it is only necessary to reset the amount of automatic throttle opening which should occur when the choke is operated. Do this by screwing down the throttle stop screw on each carburetor an equal amount until a fast idle is obtained with approximately half choke. This will give the necessary cold start throttle opening. After this is done, ensure that when the choke is fully released the throttles are closed.

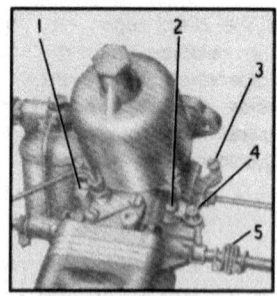

1. Slow-run valve. 2. Top plate securing screw. 3. Jet adjusting screw. 4. Throttle stop lever screw. 5. Throttle shaft interconnection clip.

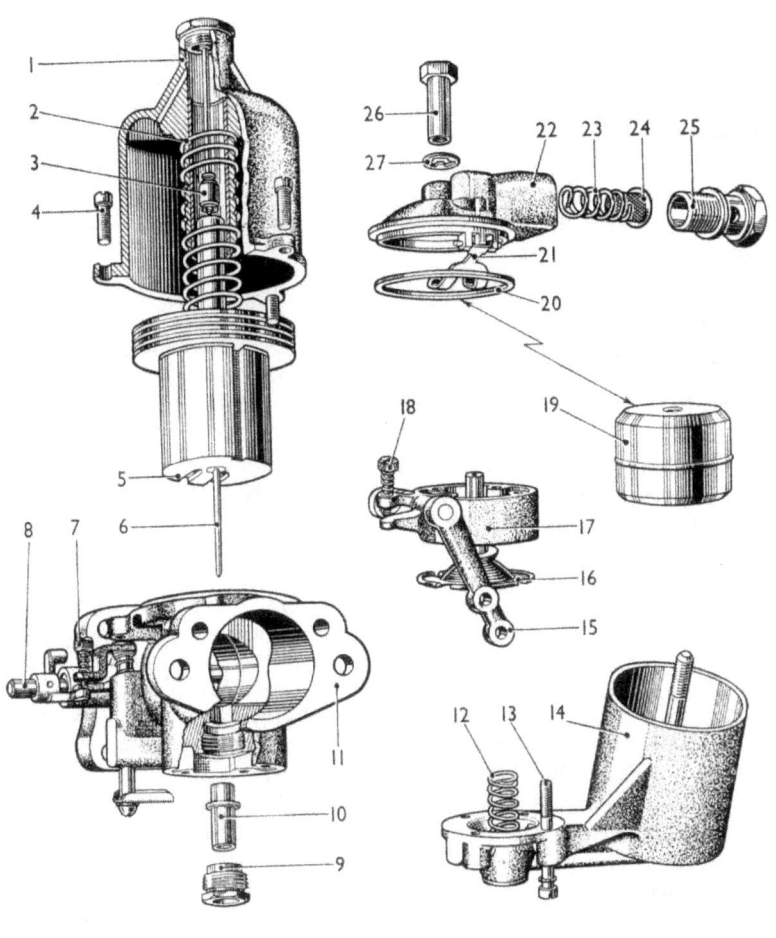

1. Suction chamber.
2. Piston spring.
3. Hydraulic damper.
4. Suction chamber screw.
5. Piston.
6. Needle.
7. Throttle stop lever adjusting screw.
8. Throttle spindle.
9. Jet screw.
10. Jet bearing.
11. Carburetter body.
12. Jet return spring.
13. Float chamber securing screw.
14. Float chamber.
15. Jet hand control lever.
16. Jet and diaphragm.
17. Diaphragm casing.
18. Jet adjusting screw.
19. Float.
20. Cover joint washer.
21. Float lever.
22. Float chamber cover.
23. Filter spring.
24. Filter.
25. Inlet union.
26. Float chamber cover screw.
27. Fibre washer.

In this installation item 15 is at the rear of the carburetter.

Defects in Operation

Since the jet of the H.D. carburetor is fed through its center and has no glands, leakage can only be caused by an insecure fit of the jet cup, an imperfect seal of the diaphragm, either at its outer edge, where it is compressed between the float-chamber and the diaphragm casing, or at its inner edge, where it is fitted to the jet, or by fracture of the diaphragm. Leakage at the outer edge may be cured by tightening the float-chamber securing screws (6) but fracture, or leaking at the inner edge will probably call for a new jet assembly.

The jet may also stick, either up or down, due to dirt between it and its bearing (2), or due to corrosion. The cure is to remove the parts by undoing the jet screw (3), clean and refit.

THERMO-CARBURETOR
(Fitted from Engine No. 29D/U/H2864)

The enrichment apparatus to assist cold starting is, in effect, an auxiliary carburation system. The main body casting (36) containing a solenoid-operated valve and fuel metering system is attached by means of a ducted mounting arm to the base of the main carburetor fuel inlet.

The auxiliary carburetor forms, therefore, a separate unit additional to the normal float-chamber, but drawing its fuel supply directly from it. Fuel is supplied to the base of the jet (29) which is obstructed to a greater or lesser degree by the tapered slidable needle (25).

When the device is in action air is drawn from the atmosphere through the air intake (26) and thence through the passage (28), being mixed with fuel as it passes the jet (29). The mixture is thence carried upwards past the shank of the needle (25) through the passage (37) and so past the aperture provided between the valve (33) and its seating (35). From here it passes directly to the induction manifold through the external feed pipe shown.

The device is brought into action by energizing the winding of the solenoid (31) from the terminal screws (30). The centrally located iron core (32) is thus raised magnetically, carrying with it the ball-jointed disc valve (33) against the load of the small conical spring (34) and thus uncovering the aperture provided by the seating (35). Considering the function of the slidable needle (25), it will be seen that this is loaded upwards in its open position by means of the slight compression spring (24) which abuts against a disc (23), attached to the shank of the needle. The needle continues upwards through the vertically adjustable stop (22) in which it is slidably mounted and it finally terminates in an enlarged head.

Depression within the space surrounding the spring (24) is directly derived from that prevailing in the induction tract, and this exerts a downward force upon the disc (23), which is provided with an adequate clearance with its surrounding bore. This tends to overcome the load of the spring (24) and to move the needle downwards,

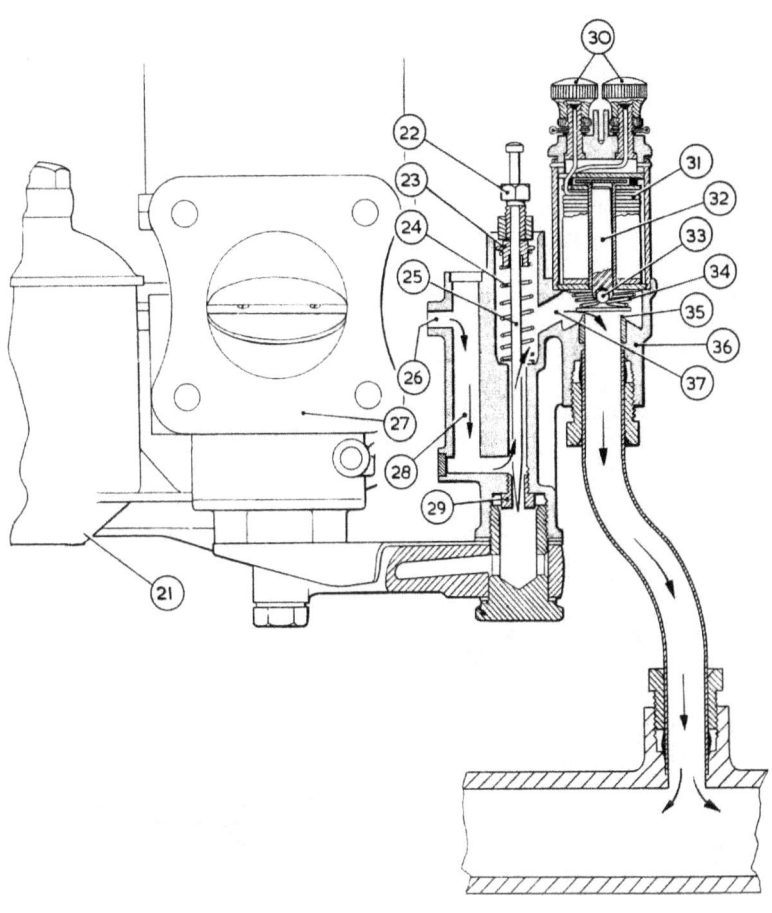

21. Float chamber.
22. Stop screw.
23. Disc.
24. Spring.
25. Needle.
26. Air intake.
27. Carburetter body.
28. Air passage.
29. Jet.
30. Terminals.
31. Solenoid.
32. Core.
33. Valve.
34. Conical spring.
35. Valve seating.
36. Body casting.
37. Passage.

thus increasing the obstruction afforded by the tapered section which enters the jet (29).

The purpose of this device is to provide two widely different degrees of enrichment, the one corresponding to idling or light cruising conditions and the other to conditions of open throttle or full-power operation. In effect, under the former conditions the high induction depression prevailing will cause the disc (23) to be drawn downwards, drawing the tapered needle into the jet (29), while under the latter, the lower depression existing in the induction tract will permit the collar to maintain its upward position with the needle withdrawn from the jet. The only adjustment provided is the needle stop screw (22) which limits the degree of movement provided for the needle assembly.

The size and degree of taper of the lower end of the needle (25), the diameter of the disc (23), and the load provided by the spring (24) are not adjustable.

The solenoid (31) is energized by means of a thermostatically operated switch housed within the cylinder head water jacket. This is arranged to bring the apparatus into action at temperatures below 86-95°F. (30-35°C.).

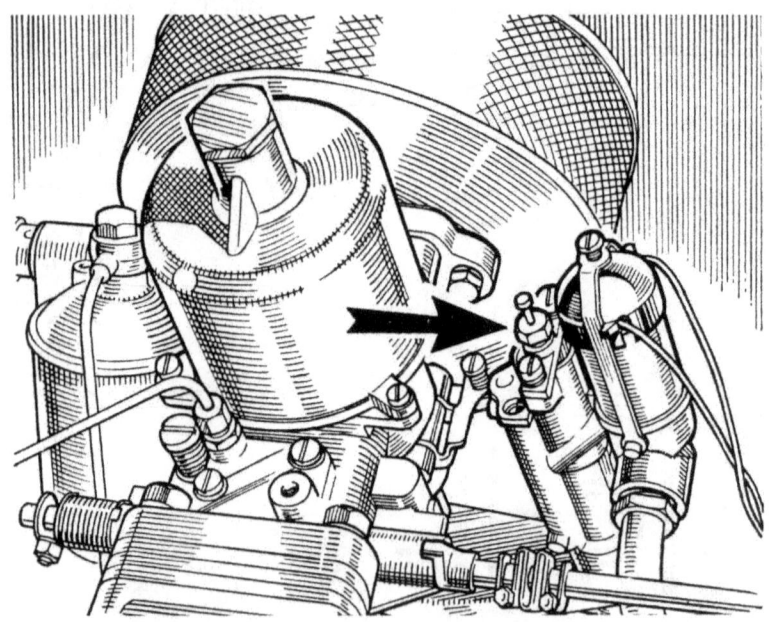

The needle stop screw indicated by the arrow adjusts the mixture strength of the thermo-carburetter.

Centering the Jet

Adjustment of the auxiliary carburetor is confined to the top screw which limits the downwards movement of the needle. Anti-clockwise rotation of the stop screw will raise the needle and increase the mixture strength, while rotation in the opposite direction will have the opposite effect.

An approximate guide to its correct adjustment is provided by energizing the solenoid when the engine has already attained its normal running temperature. The stop screw should then be so adjusted that the mixture is distinctly although not excessively rich, that is to say, until the exhaust gases are seen to be discernibly black in color, but just short of the point where the engine commences to run with noticeable irregularity.

In order to energize the solenoid under conditions when the thermostatic switch will normally have broken the circuit, it is merely necessary to short-circuit the terminal of the thermostatic switch directly to ground or, by means of a separate wire, ground the solenoid terminal which is connected to the switch (Blue—White Wire).

NOTE—Should difficulty be experienced when starting from cold on the next occasion, unscrew the stop screw (22) one or two flats only.

MODIFIED STARTING JET NEEDLE SPRING

To improve starting characteristics, the green spring (24), fitted to the starting jet needle has been changed to a blue spring (Part No. AUC1041) commencing at engine No. 3664. It is recommended that all engines between 2864 and 3664 be checked and that the blue spring be fitted if it is not already incorporated.

Mk. III   SERIES BJ8

CARBURETORS

1. *Jet adjusting nut*
2. *Throttle adjusting screw.*
3. *Fast idle adjusting screw.*
4. *Jet locking nut.*
5. *Float chamber securing nut.*
6. *Jet link.*
7. *Jet head.*
8. *Vacuum ignition take-off.*

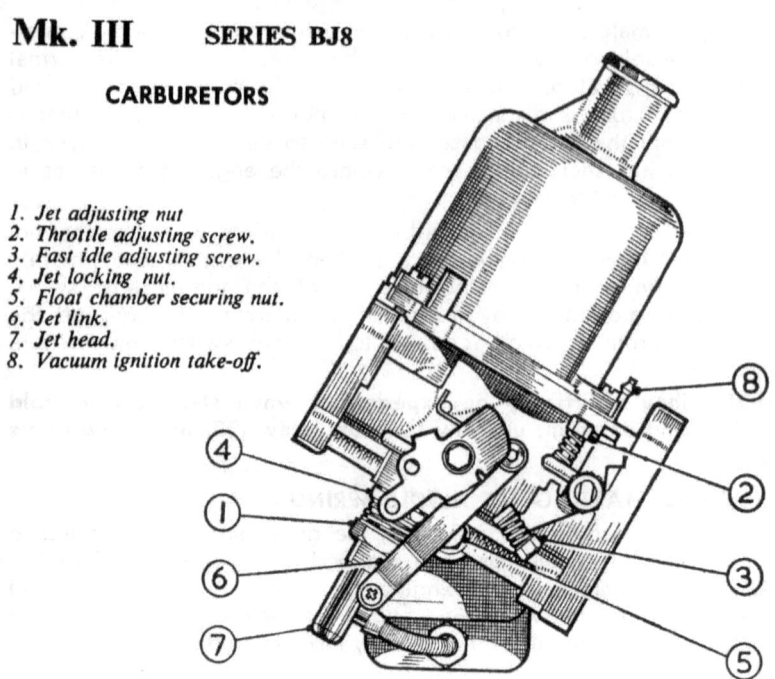

Healey 3000 Mk. II

The carburetors fitted to the Healey 3000 Mk. II are triple S.U. type H.S.4. Each carburetor is mounted on an individual manifold secured to the cylinder head by three studs and nuts, and interconnected by an external balance pipe running above the manifolds.

The H.S.4. carburetor is of the automatically expanding choke type in which the size of the main air passage (or choke) over the jet, and the effective area of the jet, are variable according to the degree of throttle opening used on the engine against the prevailing road conditions (which may differ widely from light cruising to heavy pulling). Therefore, to serve the complete throttle range a single jet only is used, being a simple metal tube sliding in a single bearing bush, fed by fuel along a small diameter nylon tube leading direct from the base of the float-chamber. The jet is varied in effective area by a tapered fuel metering needle.

Adjustments

Slow-running is governed by the setting of the jet adjusting nuts and the throttle adjusting screws, all of which must be correctly set and synchronized if satisfactory results are to be obtained.

Before blaming the carburetor setting for incorrect slow-running make certain that the trouble is not caused by badly adjusted distributor contact points, faulty plugs, incorrect valve clearance, or faulty valves and springs.

Slow running adjustment and synchronization

After the first 1,000 miles (1,600 km.) or so when the engine is fully run in, the slow running may require adjustment. This must only be carried out when the engine has reached its normal running temperature.

As the needle size is determined during engine development, tuning of the carburetors is confined to correct idling setting. Slacken the actuating arms on the throttle spindle inter-connection. Close all throttles fully by unscrewing the throttle adjusting screws, then open each throttle by screwing down the idling adjustment screws one turn.

Remove pistons and suction chambers, and disconnect the jet control cables. Screw the jet adjusting nuts until each jet is flush with the bridge of its carburetor, or as near to this as possible (all jets being in the same relative position to the bridge of their respective carburetors). Replace the pistons and suction chamber assemblies, and check that the pistons fall freely on to the bridge of the carburetors (by use of the piston lifting pins). Turn down the jet adjusting nut two complete turns (12 flats).

Re-start the engine, and adjust the throttle adjusting screws to give the desired idling speed, by moving each throttle adjusting screw an equal amount. By listening to the hiss in the intakes, adjust the throttle adjusting screws until the intensity of the hiss is similar on all intakes. This will synchronize the throttle setting.

When this is satisfactory, the mixture should be adjusted by screwing each jet adjusting nut up or down by the same amount, until the fastest idling speed is obtained consistent with even firing. During this adjusting, it is necessary that the jets are pressed upwards to ensure that they are in contact with the adjusting nuts.

As the mixture is adjusted the engine will probably run faster, and it may therefore be necessary to unscrew the throttle adjusting screws a little, each by the same amount, to reduce the speed.

Now check the mixture strength by lifting the piston of the front carburetor by approximately 1/32 in. (.75 mm.) when if:

(a) the engine speed increases, this indicates that the mixture strength of the front carburetor is too rich.

(b) the engine speed immediately decreases, this indicates that the mixture strength of the front carburetor is too weak.

(c) the engine speed momentarily increases very slightly, then the mixture strength of the front carburetor is correct.

Repeat the operation at the center and rear carburetors, and after adjustment re-check the front carburetor, since all carburetors are inter-dependent.

When the mixture is correct the exhaust note should be regular and even. If it is irregular with a splashy type of misfire and colorless exhaust, the mixture is too weak. If there is a regular or rhythmical type of misfire in the exhaust beat, together with a blackish exhaust, then the mixture is too rich.

The carburetor throttle on each carburetor is operated by a lever and pin, with the pin working in a forked lever attached to the throttle spindle. A clearance exists between the pin and the fork, which must be maintained when the throttle is closed and the engine idling, to prevent any load from the accelerator linkage being transferred to

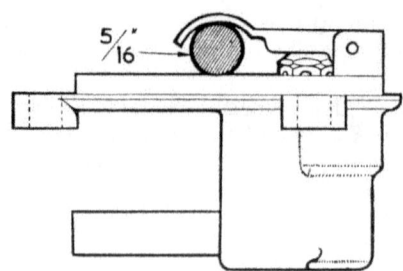

the throttle butterfly and spindle.

To set this clearance: with the throttle shaft levers free on the throttle shaft, put a .012 in. (.305 mm.) feeler between each throttle shaft stop at the top and the carburetor heat shield. Move each throttle shaft lever downwards in turn until the lever pin rests lightly on the lower arm of the fork in the carburetor throttle lever. Tighten the clamp bolt of the throttle shaft lever at this position. When all three carburetors have been dealt with, remove the feelers. The pins on the throttle shafts should then have clearance in the forks.

Re-connect the choke cables, ensuring that the jet heads return against the lower face of the jet adjusting nuts when the choke control is pushed fully in.

Pull out the mixture control knob on the dash panel to its maximum movement without moving the carburetor jets (about ⅝ in.) (15.87 mm.) and adjust the fast idle cam screws to give an engine speed of about 1,000 r.p.m. when hot.

The Float-chamber

The position of the forked lever in the float-chamber must be such that the lever of the float (and therefore the height of the fuel at the jet) is correct.

This is checked by inserting a 5/16 in. (7.94 mm.) round bar between the forked lever and the machined lip of the float-chamber lid. The prongs of the lever should rest on the bar when the needle is on its seating. If this is not so, the lever should be reset at the point where the prongs meet the shank. Care must be taken not to bend the shank, which must be perfectly flat and at right angles to the needle when it is on its seating.

Jet centering

To check the jet for concentricity with the jet needle, set the jet head and the jet adjusting nut in the uppermost position, lift the suction piston with the piston lifting pin and allow the piston to fall. It should fall freely and a definite soft metallic click will be heard as the base of the piston strikes the jet bridge.

If this does not happen with the jet raised, but does occur when the jet is lowered, the jet bearing and jet must be recentered as follows: —

Disconnect the link between the jet head and carburetor lever by removing the small Phillips retaining screw from the jet head.

Unscrew the union securing the jet feed tube into the base of the float chamber and withdraw the jet from the jet bearing, complete with feed tube.

Unscrew the jet adjusting nut and remove the lock spring; screw up the nut to its fullest extent and refit the jet head and feed tube.

Slacken the jet locking nut until the jet bearing is just free to rotate with finger pressure. Remove the piston damper from the top of the suction chamber body and gently press down the piston on to its stop.

Tighten the jet locking nut, at the same time ensuring that the jet head is held firmly in its uppermost position and at its correct angular relation to the float chamber.

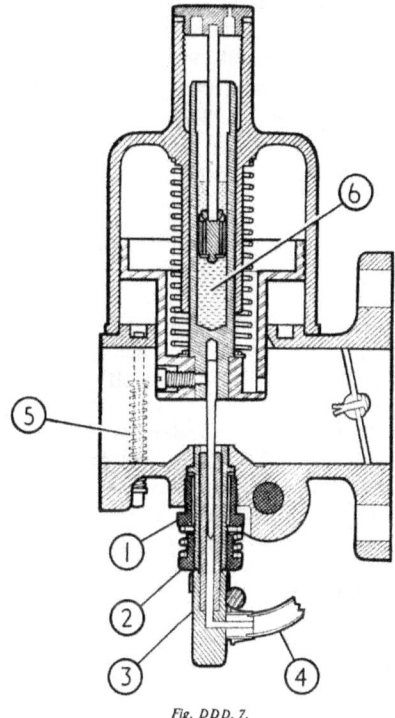

Fig. DDD. 7.

1. Jet locking nut.
2. Jet adjusting nut.
3. Jet head.
4. Feed tube from float chamber
5. Piston lifting pin.
6. Damper reservoir.

Repeat the check for concentricity both with the jet raised and lowered. If the result is not satisfactory the recentering operation must be repeated until the correct result is obtained.

When the operation is completed, replace the adjusting nut lock spring and the jet operating link.

This adjustment is best effected with the carburetors removed from the engine.

Float needle sticking

If the engine runs unevenly, apparently through lack of fuel, when there is plenty in the tank and the pump is working properly, the probable cause is a sticking float needle. An easy test for this is to disconnect the pipe from the electric pump to the carburetor and switch the ignition on and off quickly while the end of the pipe is directed onto a pad of cloth or into a container.

If fuel is delivered, starvation is almost certainly being caused by the float needle sticking to its seating, and the float chamber lid(s) should therefore be removed and the needle and seating cleaned and refitted.

At the same time it will be advisable to clean out the entire fuel feed system as this trouble is caused by foreign matter in the fuel, and unless this is removed it is likely to recur. It is of no use whatever renewing any of the component parts of the carburetor(s), and the only cure is to make sure that the fuel tank and pipe lines are entirely free from any kind of foreign matter or sticky substance capable of causing this trouble.

Piston sticking

The piston assembly comprises the suction disc and the piston forming the choke, into which is inserted the hardened and ground piston road which engages in a bearing in the center of the suction chamber and in which is, in turn, inserted the jet needle. The piston road running in the bearing is the only part which is in actual contact with any other part, the suction disc, piston, and needle all having suitable clearances to prevent sticking. If sticking does occur the whole assembly should be cleaned carefully and the piston rod lubricated with a spot of thin oil. No oil must be applied to any other part except the piston rod. A sticking piston can be ascertained by removing the piston damper and lifting the piston by pressing the piston lifting pin; the piston should come up quite freely and fall back smartly onto its seating when released. On no account should the piston return spring be stretched or its tension altered in an attempt to improve its rate of return.

FLOAT CHAMBER OVERFLOW PIPES

Flexible plastic overflow pipes were fitted to each carburetor float chamber from Power Unit No. 29E-H-1092. The float chamber lids were modified to incorporate short overflow nozzles on to which the flexible pipes are a push fit. The overflow pipes may be fitted with the modified lids to earlier 3000 Mk. II cars.

CARBURETORS WITH NYLON FLOATS

Carburetors fitted to later 3000 Mk. II cars incorporated float chambers equipped with nylon floats in place of the metal floats used previously. The nylon floats are integral with the float levers which are attached to the float chamber lids. The nylon float and lever assembly may be interchanged with the earlier metal float and separate lever. Red aluminum tags were used for a time to identify carburetors modified in this way.

To check the float lever, hold the float chamber lid and float assembly upside down and place a ⅛ in. (3.18 mm.) diameter bar across the diameter of the machined lip of the float chamber lid, parallel with the float lever hinge pin, and under the float lever. The face of the float lever should just rest on the bar when the needle valve is fully on its seating. If it does not do this, carefully reset the angle made between the straight portion of the float lever and its hinge until the correct position is obtained.

REVISED LOCATION OF FUEL PUMP

From Car No. 17547 (BN7) and 17352 (BT7) the fuel pump and fuel lines were transferred from the left-hand side to the right-hand side of the car. The repositioning of these components isolates them from the exhaust system and diminishes any possibility of fuel vaporization. This change involved the introduction of new fuel pipes between the tank and the pump, and between the pump and the flexible pipe leading to the carburetors, new petrol pipe fittings, and associated body modifications.

On the BT7 the fuel pump is now accessible when the right-hand rear seat pan has been removed.

Access to the fuel pump on the BN7 is obtained in the same way as before although it is now located on the right-hand side.

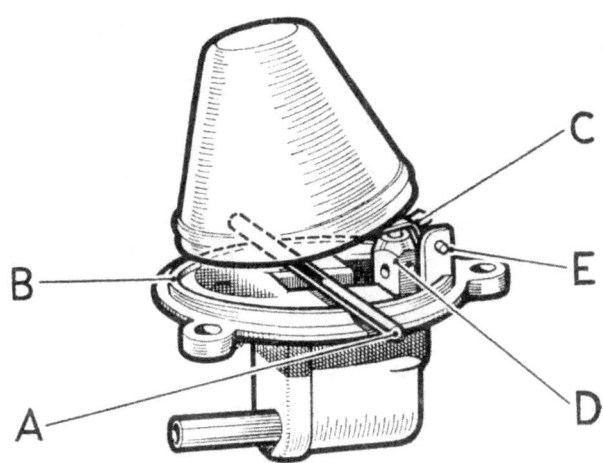

Checking the nylon float level.

A. ⅛ in. diameter bar. C. Float lever resetting point.
B. Machined lip. D. Needle valve assembly.
  E. Hinge pin.

CONVERTIBLE MODEL CARBURETORS

The Austin-Healey 3000 Mk. II Sports Convertible (Series BJ7) is equipped with twin S.U. carburetors, type HS6. Each carburetor is attached by four studs and nuts to a detachable one-piece six port induction manifold. The carburetor float chambers incorporate nylon floats and are fitted with flexible overflow pipes.

AUSTIN HEALEY SPRITE AND MG MIDGET

The Sprite Mk I uses a different carburetor than either the Sprite Mk II or the M.G. Midget. The difference, however, is only in casting construction. The early Sprite uses the S.U. H I unit, which has a separate float bowl attached to the main carburetor body by means of a feed-through screw and thick rubber grommet. Later Sprites and all M.G. Midgets use the S.U. model HS 2, which has the float chamber attached to the main carburetor body as an integral part of the casting.

No.	Description
1.	Body—bare—front.
1A.	Body—bare—rear.
4.	Suction chamber and piston assembly.
5.	Oil damper assembly.
8.	Fibre washer—oil damper cap.
10.	Securing screw—suction chamber.
11.	Spring washer—D/C—screw.
12.	Jet needle.
13.	Jet needle locking screw.
15.	Jet with head.
16.	Jet sealing nut.
17.	Jet adjusting nut.
19.	Jet adjusting lock spring.
20.	Jet sealing ring—brass.
21.	Jet sealing ring—cork.
22.	Jet bearing copper washer—bottom half bearing
23.	Jet bearing—bottom half.
24.	Jet gland washer—cork.
25.	Jet gland washer—brass.
26.	Jet gland spring.
27.	Jet bearing—top half.
28.	Jet bearing copper washer—top half bearing.
29.	Jet return spring.
34.	Jet lever.
35.	Jet link.
37.	Nut (2 BA).
38.	Washer.
39.	Pivot pin—short.
39A.	Pivot pin—jet link.
41.	Pivot pin—jet lever to stirrup.
41A.	Screw—cable clamp.
41B	Starlock washer—jet link.
41C.	Starlock washer—link rod.
42.	Split pin.
45.	Link rod.
45A.	Stirrup—connecting jet lever.
46.	Float-chamber—bare—front.
46A.	Float-chamber—bare—rear.
47.	Float-chamber lid.
48.	Float-chamber lid washer.
49.	Overflow pipe—front.
49A.	Overflow pipe—rear.
50.	Serrated fibre washer—cap nut.
51.	Aluminium packing washer.
52.	Float.
53.	Float needle and seat assembly.
55.	Float hinged lever.
56.	Float hinged lever pin.
64.	Cap nut—float lid.
66.	Holding-up bolt—float—chamber.
68.	Washer—steel—holding-up bolt.
68A.	Rubber grommet—holding-up bolt.
81.	Throttle spindle—front.
81A.	Throttle spindle—rear.
82.	Throttle disc.
83.	Throttle disc screw.
86.	Return spring—throttle—front.
87.	End clip.
88.	Anchor plate.
89.	Throttle lever.
90.	Bolt (2 BA).
91.	Taper pin.
92.	Throttle stop—front.
92A.	Throttle stop—rear.
93.	Adjusting screw.
94.	Lock spring—screw.
95	Rocker lever—front.
96.	Bolt—pivot—front.
96A.	Spring washer—pivot bolt.
96B.	Aluminium washer—cam.
99.	Coupling—folded.
100.	Connecting rod—throttle.
101.	Bolt (4 BA).
102.	Nut (4 BA).
103.	Washer (4 BA).

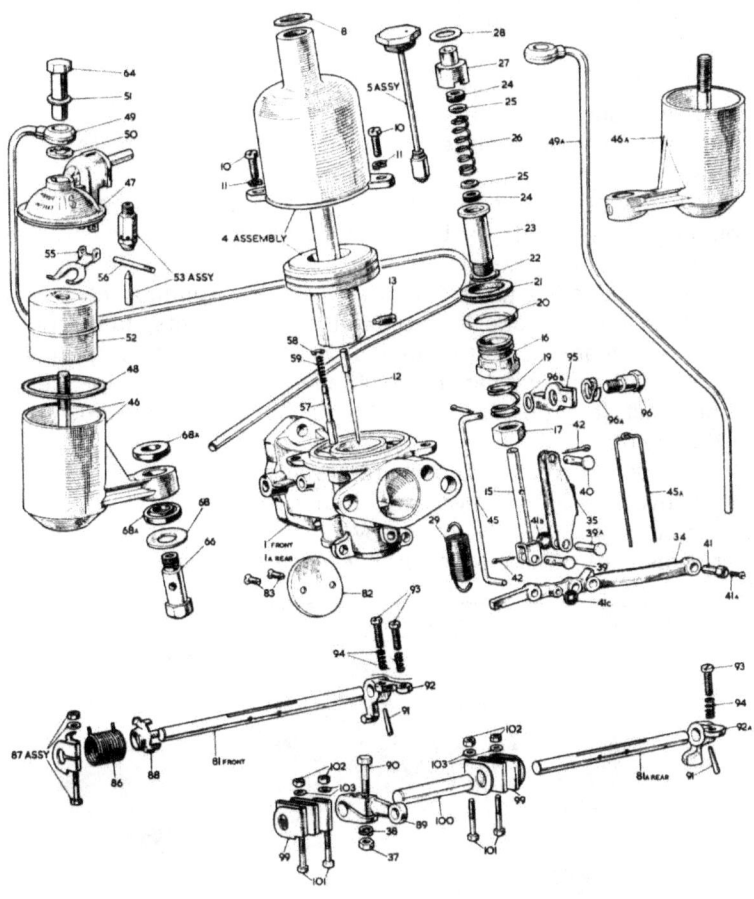

SPRITE (H.I.) CARBURETORS

The two S.U. type H.I. carburetors are of the variable-jet type, fitted with twin 'Pancake' air cleaners.

A damper is provided in each carburetor, consisting of a plunger and non-return valve attached to the oil cap nut, and operates in the hollow piston rod which is partly filled with oil. Its function is to give a slightly enriched mixture on acceleration by controlling the rise of the piston and to prevent piston flutter.

ADJUSTMENT

It is first essential to run the engine until it has attained its normal running temperature before commencing any mixture or slow-running adjustments.

The slow-running is governed by the setting of the jet adjusting screws and the throttle stop screws, all of which must be correctly set and synchronized if satisfactory results are to be obtained.

The throttles are interconnected by a coupling shaft and spring coupling clips which enable them to be correctly synchronized when adjustments take place.

Before blaming the settings for bad slow-running make quite sure that it is not due to badly set contact points, faulty plugs, bad valve clearance setting or faulty valves and valve springs.

Good slow-running cannot be obtained if the setting for the jets is incorrect. It is therefore advisable to commence any adjustments at this point.

In order to adjust the carburetors successfully it is necessary to remove the air cleaners and intake pipe assembly from the carburetors and engine valve cover and make sure the pistons work freely and the jets are properly centered (see below).

1 & 3. *Slow running adjustment screws.* 2. *Throttle mixture control interconnecting lever adjustor.*

Adjusting the Jets

(1) Slacken off the pinch-bolt of one of the spring coupling clips locating the interconnecting shaft to the throttle spindles and also release the two screws securing the choke spring to the jet levers, so that each carburetor can be operated independently.

(2) Release the throttle lever adjusting screws until both throttles are completely closed.

(3) Turn the throttle lever adjusting screw for the rear carburetor clockwise until it is just touching the web on the body and then give it one full turn. This will set the rear carburetor for fast idling and leave the front one out of action. This can be ensured further by lifting the front carburetor piston a matter of ½ in. (13 mm.).

(4) With the engine running, set the jet adjusting screw for the rear carburetor so that a mixture strength is obtained which will give the best running speed for this throttle opening, taking care to see that the jet head is kept in firm contact with the adjusting nut the whole time.

(5) The correctness or otherwise of this setting can be checked by raising the suction piston with a small screwdriver, or similar instrument to the extent of 1/32 in. (.8 mm). This should cause a very slight momentary increase in the engine speed without impairing the evenness of running in any way.

If this operation has the effect of stopping the engine it is an indication that the mixture setting is too weak (lean). If an appreciable speed increase occurs and continues to occur when the piston is raised as much as ¼ in. (6 mm.) it is an indication that the mixture is too rich.

(6) When the rear carburetor mixture setting has been carried out correctly release its throttle adjusting screw so that it is clear of the stop and the throttle is completely closed, and lift the piston ½ in. (13 mm.) to render it inoperative. Then repeat the jet-adjusting operations on the front carburetor.

(7) When both carburetors are correctly adjusted individually for mixture strength the throttles of each should be set so as to give the required slow-running and synchronization.

Slow-running and Synchronization

Screw each throttle lever adjusting screw so that its end is only just making contact with the web on the body, then give each screw one full turn exactly.

Start the engine, which will now idle on the fast side.

Unscrew each throttle lever adjusting screw an equal amount, a fraction of a turn at a time until the desired slow-running speed is achieved.

Correct synchronization can be checked by listening at each carburetor air intake in turn through a length of rubber tube and notice of the noise produced by the incoming air is the same in both. Any variation in intensity of the sound indicates that one throttle is set more widely open than the other — the louder sound indicates the throttle with the greater opening.

When the same intensity of sound is produced by both carburetors the intercoupling shaft clip should be tightened up firmly to ensure that the throttles work in unison.

Since the delivery characteristics, when both carburetors are operating together, vary somewhat from those existing when each is working separately it will be found necessary to check them again for correctness of mixture strength by lifting the pistons in turn as described in 'Adjusting the jets,' making such adjustments of the jet adjusting nuts as are required to balance the mixture strength and to ensure that it is not too rich.

Another method of synchronization is to employ a visual vacuum indicator such as the "Unisyn", available at sportscar accessory houses or parts departments of many dealerships. These units are simple in construction and adjustable over a wide range of vacuum. The technique is to place the base of the instrument firmly against the intake of the first carburetor and regulate the flow through the base by means of an adjusting screw until the float is centered in the tube. Then move the instrument to the second carburetor. If the float changes relative position, up or down, it indicates that the throttle setting is at variance with that of the first carburetor. Regulating the throttle lever adjusting screw to bring the float back to center accomplishes synchronization.

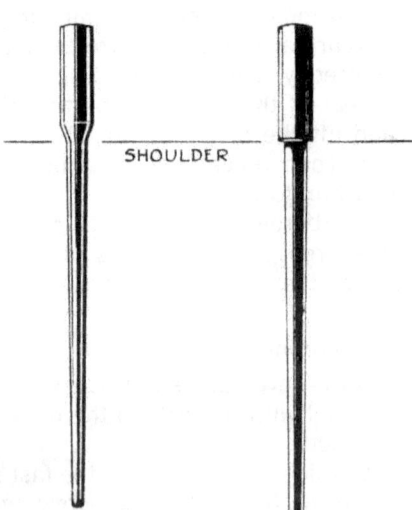

The shoulder of the needle should be flush with the underface of the piston. Two types of shoulder are in use and the correct datum point for each is shown.

Fitting New Needles

If the road performance is not satisfactory after the above adjustments have been made, larger or smaller needles may be necessary.

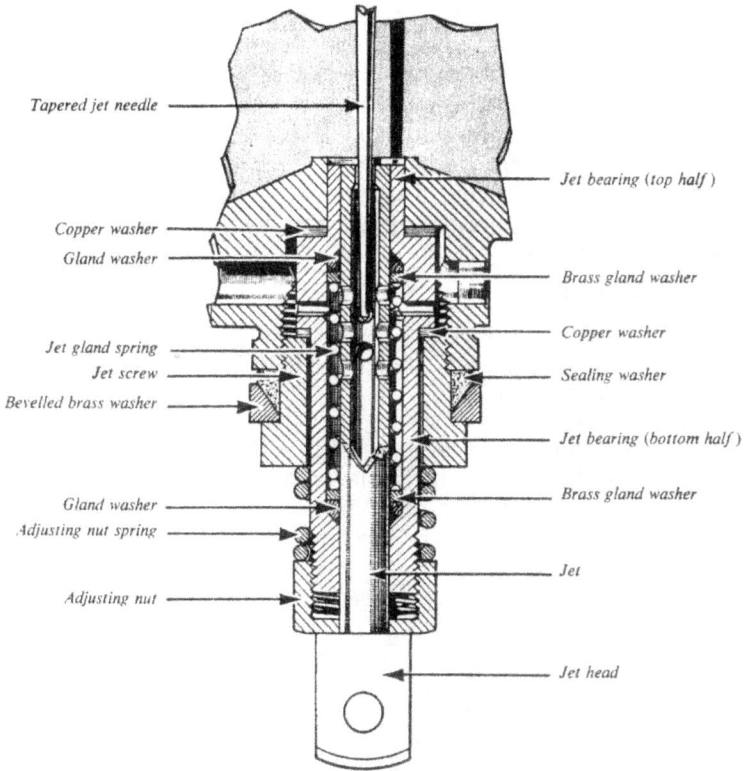

To change the needles, remove the screws and lift off the suction chambers, having marked them to ensure refitting to their respective units. Remove the pistons.

Unscrew the screw at the side of each piston tube and withdraw the needles.

Fit the new needles: a needle should be fitted with its shoulder flush with the face of the piston.

Centering a Jet

First remove the clevis pin at the base of the jet which attaches the jet head to the jet operating lever; withdraw the jet completely, and remove the adjusting nut and adjusting nut spring. Replace the adjusting nut without its spring and screw it up to the highest position. Slide the jet into position until the jet head is against the base of the adjusting nut. When this has been done, feel if this piston is perfectly free by lifting it up with the finger with the dashpot piston removed. If it is not, slacken the jet sealing nut and manipulate the lower part of the assembly, including the projecting part of the bottom half jet bearing, adjusting nut and jet head. Make sure that this assembly is now slightly loose. The piston should then rise and fall quite easily as the needle is now able to move the jet into the required central position. The jet sealing nut should now be tightened and a check made to determine that this piston is still quite free. If it is not found to be so, the jet sealing nut should be slackened again and the operation repeated. When complete freedom of the piston is achieved the jet adjusting nut should be replaced. The adjusting nut should now be screwed back to its original position.

Experience shows that a large percentage of carburetors returned for correction have had jets removed and incorrectly centered on replacement.

The Float-chamber

The position of the forked lever in the float-chamber must be such that the level of the float (and therefore the height of the fuel at the jet) is correct.

This is checked by inserting a 7/16 in. (11.11 mm.) round bar between the forked lever and the machined lip of the float-chamber lid. The prongs of the lever should just rest on the bar when the needle is on its seating. If this is not so, the lever should be reset at the point where the prongs meet the shank. Care must be taken not to bend the shank which must be perfectly flat and at right angles to the needle when it is on its seating.

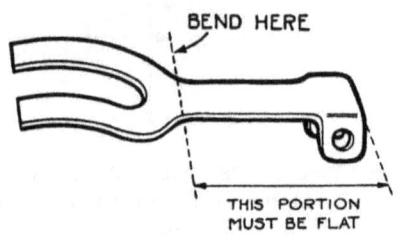

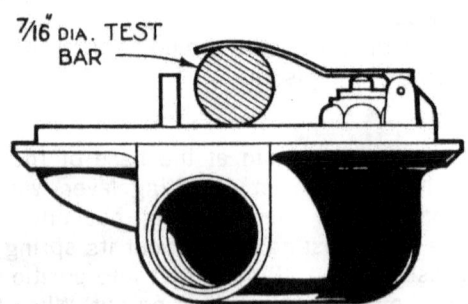

SOURCES OF TROUBLE

Piston Sticking

The piston assembly comprises the suction disc and the piston forming the choke into which is inserted the hardened and ground piston rod which engages in a bearing in the center of the suction chamber and in which is, in turn, inserted the jet needle.

The piston rod running in the bearing is the only part which is in actual contact with any other part, the suction disc, piston, and needle all having suitable clearances to prevent sticking. If sticking does occur the whole assembly should be cleaned carefully and the piston rod lubricated with a drop of thin oil. No oil must be applied to any other part except the piston rod. A sticking piston can be ascertained by removing the dashpot piston damper, inserting a finger in the air intake and lifting the piston, which should come up quite freely and fall back smartly onto its seating when released.

Water or Dirt in the Carburetor

When this is suspected lift the piston: the jet can then be seen; flood the carburetor and watch the jet; if fuel does not flow through freely there is a blockage. To remedy this, start the engine, open up the throttle, and block up the air inlet momentarily without shutting the throttle, keep the throttle open until the engine starts to race. This trouble seldom arises with the S.U. owing to the size of the jet and fuel ways. When it does occur the above method will nearly always clear it. Should it not do so, the only alternative is to remove the jet.

Float-chamber Flooding

This can be revealed by fuel flowing over the float-chamber and dripping from the air inlet, and is generally caused by grit between the float chamber needle and its guide. Remove the float chamber top and withdraw the float lever by extracting its pivot pin. The needle valve will now drop out of its seating and can be checked for cleanliness. If there is no grit or foreign matter on the needle or its seating make certain that the needle is not unduly worn. Should this be the case a new needle valve and seating must be fitted.

Float Needle Sticking

If the engine stops, apparently through lack of fuel when there is plenty in the tank and the pump is working properly, the probable cause is a sticking float needle. An easy test for this is to disconnect the pipe from the fuel pump to the carburetor, turn the engine with the starter motor to check if the fuel is being delivered; if it is starvation it has almost certainly been caused by the float needle sticking to its seat, and the float chamber lid should therefore be removed, the needle and seat cleaned, and refitted. At the same time it will be advisable to clean out the entire fuel system, as this trouble is caused by foreign matter in the fuel, and unless this is removed it is likely to recur. It is of no use whatever renewing any of the component parts of the carburetor, and the only cure is to make sure that the fuel tank and pipe lines are entirely free from any kind of foreign matter or sticky substance capable of causing this trouble.

THE AIR CLEANERS

Remove the units and wash the gauze in petrol (gasoline) every 6,000 miles (9600 km.) or every 3,000 miles (4800 km.) in exceptionally dusty conditions.

When the gauze is clean and dry, re-oil it with engine oil and allow it to drain before refitting to the engine.

MODIFIED CARBURETOR DAMPER ASSEMBLIES

To allow the carburetor pistons to lift more freely avoiding restriction of performance, new hydraulic damper assemblies have been fitted in model production. The damper pistons of the new assemblies were shortened from .378 in. (9.596 mm.) to .308 in. (7.823 mm.).

These hydraulic damper assemblies (part number AUC8114) are identified by the letter 'O' stamped on the brass hexagon caps. They can be fitted, with advantage, to earlier carburetors in pairs. Alternatively, the original damper pistons may be modified be machining .070 in. (1.78 mm.) off their lower faces.

MK II AND MIDGET CARBURETORS

Construction

The HS2 carburetors are of the automatically expanding choke type in which the size of the main air passage (or choke) over the jet, and the effective area of the jet, are variable according to the degree of throttle opening used on the engine against the prevailing road conditions (which may differ widely from light cruising to heavy pulling).

To serve the complete throttle range a single jet is used, being a simple metal tube sliding in a single bearing bush, fed by fuel along a small-diameter nylon tube leading direct from the base of the float-chamber. The jet is varied in effective area by a tapered fuel metering needle sliding into it.

Piston sticking

The piston assembly comprises the suction disc and the piston forming the choke, into which is inserted the hardened and ground piston rod which engages in a bearing in the center of the suction chamber and in which is inserted the jet needle. The piston rod running in the bearing is the only part which is in actual contact with any other part, the suction disc, piston and needle all having suitable clearances to prevent sticking. If sticking does occur the whole assembly should be cleaned carefully and the piston rod lubricated with a spot of thin oil. No oil must be applied to any part except the piston rod. A sticking piston can be ascertained by removing the piston damper and lifting the piston by pressing the piston lifting pin; the piston should come up quite freely and fall back smartly onto its seating when released. On no account should the piston return spring be stretched or its tension be altered in an attempt to improve its rate of return.

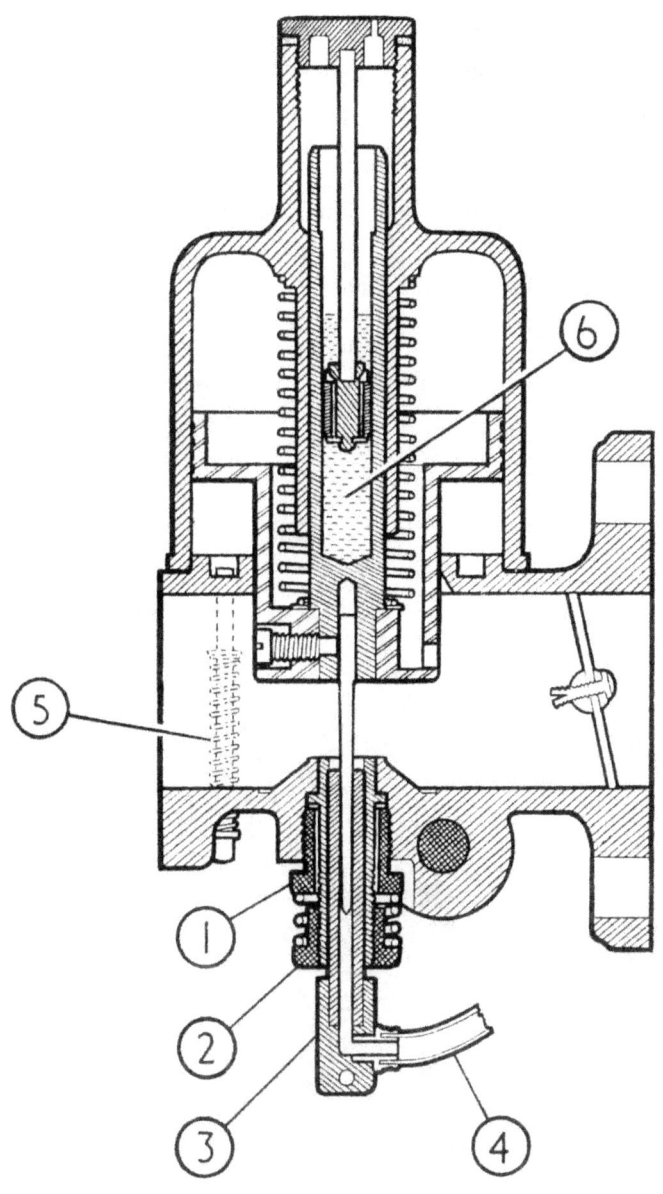

1. Jet locking nut.
2. Jet adjusting nut.
3. Jet head.
4. Nylon fuel pipe.
5. Piston lifting pin.
6. Piston damper oil well.

Water and dirt in the carburetors

Float-chamber flooding

Float needle sticking

Adjustments

For these conditions, see same headings under Sprite, H.I. Carburetor.

Slow-running and synchronization

Slacken the pinch-bolt of the delayed-action lever coupling the rear throttle spindle to the interconnecting shaft. This will permit each carburetor throttle to be set independently of the other.

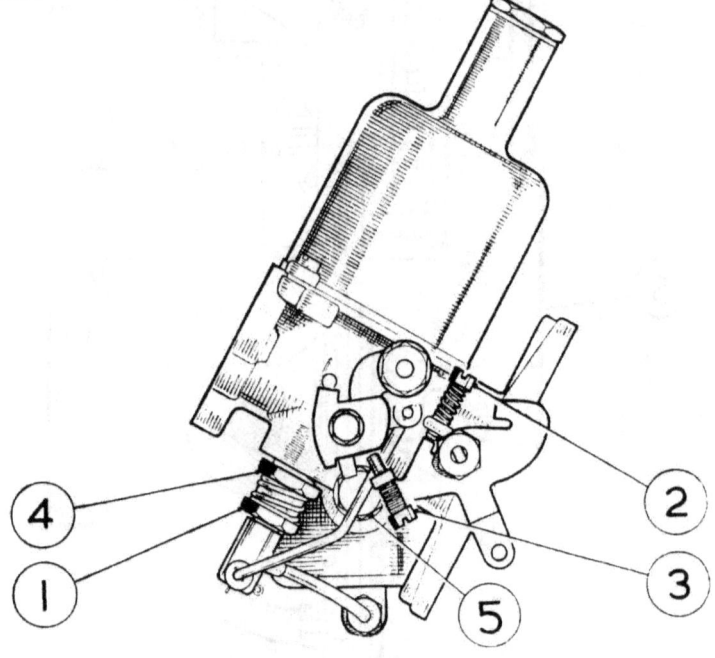

1. Jet adjusting nut.
2. Throttle adjusting screw.
3. Fast-idle adjustment screw.
4. Jet locking nut.
5. Float-chamber bolt.

Unscrew the throttle adjusting screws and screw these back until they will just hold a thin strip of paper between the end of the screw and the fixed stop web on the butterfly arm when the throttle disc is fully shut; then screw them in one complete turn.

The engine may now be started and left running until thoroughly warmed up, when it may be found necessary to readjust the throttle adjusting screws by equal amounts in either direction according to whether a higher or lower speed is required. To check for exact matching of the throttle openings it is best to listen to the air intake hiss, after first removing the air cleaners. This is most easily done by holding one end of a piece of rubber tubing against the ear and the other end against the intake of each carburetor in turn, when the intensity of the intake hiss can be gauged. The larger the throttle opening, the more intense is the intake hiss, and with this as a guide the necessary adjustments for matching can readily be made after a little experience.

Also, see "Using the Unisyn" above.

Adjusting the jets

When the degree of throttle opening has been dealt with, slacken the pinch-bolt on one of the coupling levers on the interconnecting shaft and adjust the mixture strength by moving both jet adjusting nuts the same amount. Move upwards for weakening or downwards for enriching until a satisfactory engine beat has been found which should give **the fastest idling speed consistent with even firing.**

When this has been found it may be necessary to lower the idling speed by slackening off slightly both throttle adjusting screws an equal amount.

Note that a weak idling mixture gives a 'splashy', irregular type of misfire, with a colourless exhaust, whilst a rich idling mixture gives a 'ryhthmical' or regular misfire, with a blackish exhaust.

When the mixture strength is correct on both carburetors lifting the piston by the special piston lifting pin on the side of the body casting will give uneven firing from excessive weakness on that particular carburetor.

If lifting this piston of one carburetor stops the engine and lifting that of the other does not, this indicates that the mixture on the first is set weaker than that on the second, and therefore the mixture strength on the first one should be enriched by unscrewing the jet adjusting nut one or two flats of the hexagon.

There is one occasion when the above check does not give a correct indication, and that is the rare condition when the throttle on one carburetor is set open a generous amount coupled with a weak setting of the jet adjusting nut, and the second is set the opposite way, with a rich setting of the jet adjusting nut coupled with a slight throttle opening. The overall effect will probably give a fair idling performance for the complete unit; but lifting the piston on the second carburetor will stop the engine although it is actually running rich — thus contradicting the original instruction. Also, lifting the piston on the first carburetor will not stop the engine although it is actually running weak; the lifting of the piston in this case only slightly weakens off an already markedly weak mixture and is not enough to stall the engine.

The obvious cure for such a combination of extremes is to make sure firstly (possibly by using the simple rubber stethoscope already described) that both throttles are open the same amount for idling, giving approximately the same suction on each jet.

Make sure that the jets are hard up against the bottom face of the adjusting nuts after any movement of the latter; also check the same point when reconnecting the link shaft between the jet units.

Although it is advisable, before the actual start of the tuning operation, to check that the jet adjusting nuts are all screwed the same amount downwards from the top-most position, later, when a satisfactory setting for each nut has been found giving a correct slow run, it may be that this finalized position is not exactly similar for each nut — that is, one may be two turns down and another two and a half turns down.

This apparent discrepancy is well within normal variation, and even on new carburetors may be as much as one full turn, depending on such factors as exactly similar positioning of each jet needle in the piston, etc. On worn units, where there is also the influencing factor of unequal wear on individual parts, then the variation in jet nut position may be greater, and up to two full turns down.

The throttle couping lever pinch-bolt may now be tightened, taking care to see that light pressure is put on the head of each throttle stop screw and setting the throttle opening delaying mechanism as the bolt is tightened.

Setting the throttle opening delaying mechanism

To ensure smooth acceleration when initially opening the throttle the linkage between the throttle spindles is designed to delay slightly the opening of the front carburetor throttle. This delaying mechanism is incorporated in the throttle spindle connecting rod rear coupling levers.

Connection between the two levers is made by a pin secured to the front lever operating in a hole drilled in the rear lever slightly larger in diameter than the pin, and it is this difference in diameter which allows a limited amount of free movement between the two levers to delay the opening of the front throttle.

To set this mechanism, slacken the front lever pinch-bolt and push the pin end of the lever towards the engine until the pin is just bearing against the engine side of the hole in the rear lever. Hold the levers in this position and tighten the pinch-bolt, ensuring that both throttle stop screws are bearing on the stop webs of the butterfly levers.

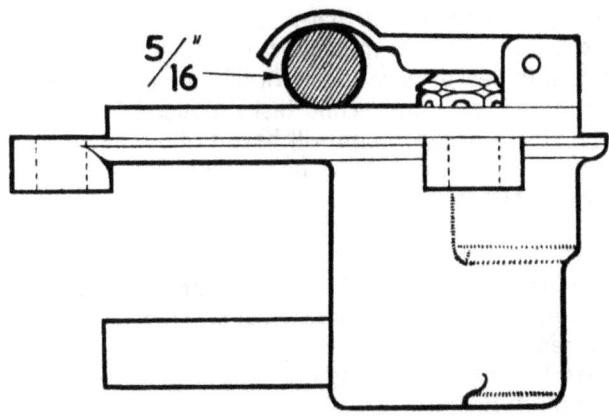

Float-chambers

The position of the float lever in the float-chamber must be such that the level of the float (and therefore the height of the fuel at the jet) is correct.

This is checked by inserting a 5/16 in. (7.94 mm.) round bar between the float lever and the machined lip of the float-chamber lid. The forked end of the lever should just rest on the bar when the needle is on its seating. If this is not so, the lever should be reset at the point where the forked end meets the shank.

Do not bend the shank, which must be perfectly flat and at right angles to the needle when it is on its seat.

Centering the jet

When the suction piston is lifted by the spring-loaded piston lifting pin it should fall freely and hit the inside jet bridge with a soft, metallic click — that is, with the jet adjusting nut (2) in its topmost position.

If this click is not audible, but is so when the test is repeated with the jet in the fully lowered position, then the jet unit requires recentering on the needle, as described below.

Disconnect the rod between the jet lever and the jet head.

Unscrew the union holding the nylon feed tube into the base of the float-chamber, and withdraw the tube and jet together. Unscrew the jet adjusting nut and remove the lock spring. Replace the adjusting nut and screw it right up to its topmost position, then replace the jet and feed tube.

Slacken off the large jet locking screw (1) until the jet bearing is just free to rotate by finger pressure.

With the damper removed and using a pencil on top of the piston rod, gently press the piston and needle down onto the jet bridge.

Tighten the jet locking screw, observing that the jet head is still in its correct angular position.

Lift the piston and check that it falls freely and evenly, hitting the jet bridge with a soft, metallic click. Then fully lower the jet and re-check to see if there is any difference in the sound of the impact; if there is and the second test produces a sharper impact sound, the centering operation will have to be repeated until successful, the nut and lock spring being replaced after the conclusion of the operation.

Removing

Remove the air cleaners. Disconnect the mixture and throttle control cables, the vacum advance pipe, and the fuel delivery hose from their respective positions on the carburetors.

Release the interconnecting coupling tension springs and the throttle stop return spring.

Remove the nuts and spring washers securing the carburetors to the manifold flanges. Lift off the assemblies as one unit. The interconnecting couplings are fitted in sleeved nuts, and when the assemblies are removed the couplings can be lifted away from both carburetors.

It should be noted that the heat shield fitted between the carburetors and the manifold flanges has gaskets, which should be renewed if the shield has been removed.

Refitting

Reverse the removal procedure when refitting.

Linkage Adjustment

See B.M.C. Mini Section for dual carb linkage adjustment information.

B.M.C. MINIS

Pickup - Traveller - Countryman Van - Riley Elf - Wolseley Hornet & Mini Cooper

General. The carburetters fitted to the Mini range as standard equipment are SU type HS2, these being 1¼ in. diameter normally having a jet size of 0·090 in. SU carburetters are of the automatically expanding choke type; the cross sectional area of the choke above the jet and the effective size of the jet is governed by the engine speed and throttle opening. A single fuel jet is used to serve the complete throttle range, this consists of a simple metal tube, sliding in a bearing bush. Fuel is fed to the jet directly from the bottom of the float chamber via a small-bore nylon tube.

The effective size of the jet is varied by a tapered needle sliding in it and thus metering the fuel supply. The needle is attached to the bottom of a sliding piston which is raised by manifold depression, exposing an increasing area of choke and also a larger jet orifice.

Where a single carburetter is fitted the needles normally used are:

Standard	EB
Rich	M
Weak	GG

On Mini Coopers, where twin carburetters are used, the carburetters are of the same type but different needles are used.

997 cc Cooper Mini	Standard	GZ
998 cc Cooper Mini	Standard	GY
970 cc Cooper S	Standard Rich Weak	AN H6 EB
1071 cc Cooper S	Standard Rich Weak	H6 3 EB
1275 cc Cooper S	Standard	M

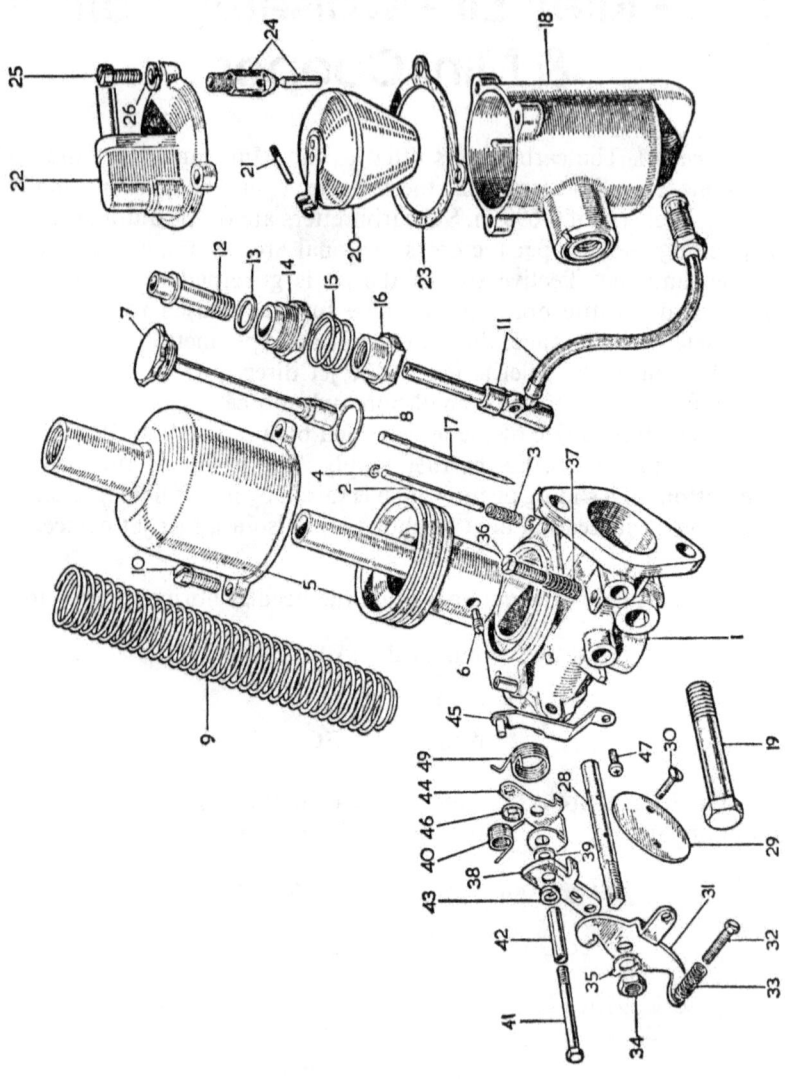

64

KEY TO CARBURETTER COMPONENTS

1. Body
2. Piston lifting pin
3. Spring for pin
4. Circlip for pin
5. Suction chamber and piston assembly
6. Needle locking screw
7. Piston damper assembly
8. Washer for damper cap (fibre)
9. Piston spring
10. Screw: suction chamber to body
11. Jet assembly
12. Jet bearing
13. Washer for jet bearing (brass)
14. Lock screw for jet bearing
15. Lock spring
16. Jet adjusting screw
17. Jet needle
18. Float-chamber body
19. Float and lever assembly
20. Lever hinge pin
21. Float-chamber lid assembly
22. Washer for lid
23. Needle and seat assembly
24. Screw: float-chamber lid to body
25. Spring washer
26. Throttle spindle
27. Throttle disc
28. Screw: throttle disc
29. Throttle lever
30. Cam stop screw
31. Spring for stop screw
34. Throttle spindle nut
35. Tab washer for nut
36. Idling stop screw
37. Spring for stop screw
38. Cam lever
39. Washer
40. Cam lever spring
41. Cam lever pivot bolt
42. Pivot bolt tube
43. Spring washer
44. Pick-up lever assembly
45. Jet link
46. Jet link retaining clip
47. Jet link securing screw
49. Spring for pick-up lever

Exploded diagram of SU carburetter type HS2.

Carburetter piston damper. To top up the piston damper, unscrew the cap (brass hexagon or knurled plastic) from the top of the suction chamber and pour in enough SAE 20 grade oil just to fill the internal well. (Fig. 2:2.) Replace cap.

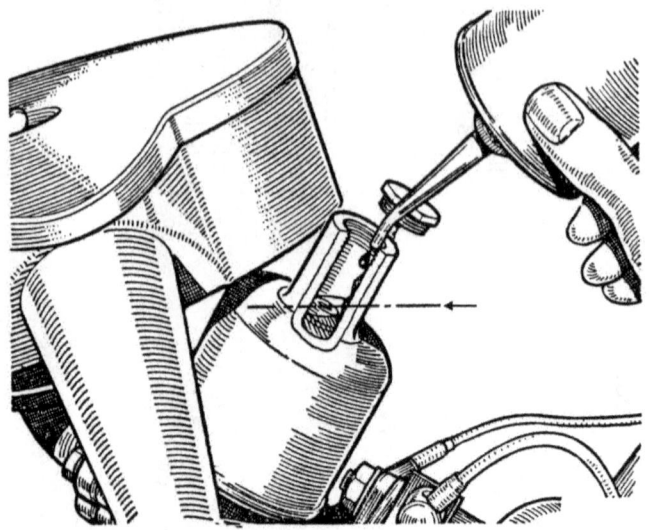

Fig. 2:2. Correct level of oil in carburetter piston damper.

Absence of oil in the piston damper will seriously interfere with the acceleration performance by allowing the choke to open too rapidly, but never use a heavy grade of oil.

The carburetter linkages should be lubricated, when servicing, with the same grade oil.

Carburetter slow running adjustment. The slow running is governed by the setting of the jet adjusting nut and the throttle adjusting screw, both of which must be correctly set and synchronized if satisfactory results are to be obtained. Before blaming the carburetter settings for bad slow running, make certain that the trouble is not caused by badly adjusted distributor contact points, faulty plugs, incorrect valve clearances, faulty valves and springs, or exhaust leaks.

To adjust the slow-running, the throttle adjusting screw is turned, clockwise to give a fast idling speed, then unscrewed a fraction of a turn at a time until the desired slow-running speed is obtained. After slow running has been adjusted, check that the 'fast-idle' adjustment screw is clear of its actuating cam by approximately $\frac{1}{64}$ in.

Carburetter jet adjustment. Uneven running of the engine, at idling speed, may indicate faulty mixture. An uneven exhaust beat with an irregular type of misfire and colourless exhaust gas indicates a weak mixture. Uneven firing of a rhythmical or regular type, coupled with a blackish exhaust gas may be due to too rich mixture. Before attempting to correct the mixture adjustment the air filter should be inspected and a new one fitted if necessary, as a dirty, blocked filter will upset the mixture. Before adjusting the jet position, the engine should be run until it attains a normal running temperature. The throttle adjusting screw should then be turned clockwise to set the throttle to a fast idling speed. (Approx. 1,000 rev/min.)

With the engine running and according to the symptoms noted, screw the jet adjusting nut, only one 'flat' of the hexagon at a time, either upwards for weakening or downwards for enriching, so that a mixture strength is obtained which will give the best running speed for this particular throttle opening, taking care that the jet head is in firm contact with the adjusting nut the whole time. In no circumstances should the jet locking nut be slackened as this will cause misalignment of the main jet, resulting in the jamming of the piston.

In order to complete the fine adjustment of the mixture, with the engine still running, raise the carburetter piston about $\frac{1}{16}$ in. by means of the piston lifting button to be found under the suction chamber. If the engine tends (1) to stall, the mixture is too weak, (2) to remain at the same speed, the mixture is only just too weak, (3) to speed up slightly when raised $\frac{1}{16}$ in. but also slow down if raised further the mixture is correct, (4) to speed up and continue to increase in speed if the piston is raised further, the mixture is too rich.

The adjusting nut is therefore turned fractionally in the appropriate direction until the correct mixture is obtained. After adjustment, the throttle adjusting screw should be reset to give the correct idling speed.

Synchronization of twin SU carburetters. Check the action of the two throttles and their connecting linkage. Set the throttle stop screw on each carburetter so that both throttles are operating in the same position and adjust the interconnecting linkage. The first step in synchronization is to screw both the jet adjusting nuts to their topmost position. If these nuts are stiff, a short spanner may be necessary for adjustment.

The engine is now started, using the mixture control ('choke') and a little throttle opening to obtain a suitable starting mixture. Once running, both throttles are set on their slow running screws so that the engine runs at a fast idle (1,000 rev/min). As the engine warms up, push in the mixture control to return the jets to their topmost position. Next, using the piston lifting button (see previous section), raise the piston of one carburetter about $\frac{1}{16}$ in. but no more. This will cause the engine to misfire and probably stall. The same will be found to occur with the other carburetter when its piston is lifted.

Returning to the first carburetter, screw the jet adjusting nut down half a turn and repeat the piston lifting technique as above, this time the engine may not misfire. (See previous section.) The other carburetter jet is adjusted the same amount and tested likewise.

The jets on both carburetters are adjusted, as for single carburetters, until lifting the piston on either of them $\frac{1}{16}$ in. results in a slight increase in engine speed. Final adjustment is by fractional movement of the jet adjusting nuts until the same increase in engine speed is achieved from each carburetter when tested.

Always adjust each jet in turn or the original balance may be lost and the procedure must then be started again.

After adjustment of the mixture, the throttle adjusting screws should be returned to the correct position for idling.

Carburetter Linkage Adjustment

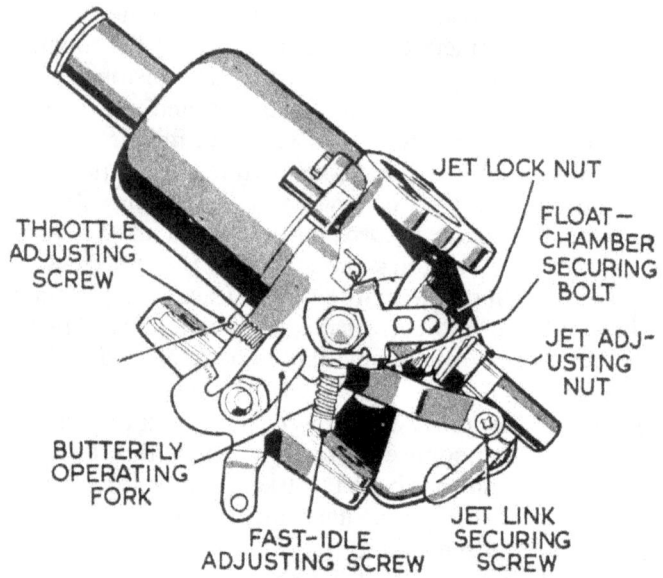

Carburetter Linkage and Adjustments.

The interconnecting shaft of the throttle linkage is connected to each carburetter throttle by means of a lever and pin attached to the shaft, with the pin operating a forked lever attached to each carburetter throttle spindle.

A clearance must exist between the pin and the fork when the throttles are closed and the engine is idling. This clearance is adjusted as follows:

(1) Loosen the throttle lever clamp screws on the interconnecting shaft.

(2) Insert a .012" feeler gauge between the throttle shaft stop and the choke interconnecting spindle.

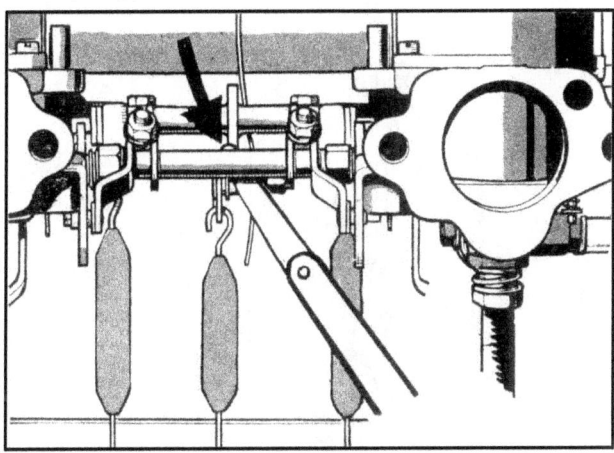

Feeler Gauge in Position Between the Throttle Lever Shaft Stop and the Choke Interconnecting Spindle, for Adjusting the Throttle Shaft Lever Pin Clearance in the Throttle Lever Forks.

(3) Press each throttle shaft lever down until the lever pin lightly contacts the lower arm of the forked lever attached to the carburetter throttle spindle in each instance.

Holding the throttle levers in this position, tighten each lever clamp bolt.

(4) Remove the feeler gauge. The throttle shaft lever pins will now have the necessary clearance in the throttle spindle lever forks.

(5) Connect the choke cable so that the jet heads are against the jet adjusting nuts when the choke control or mixture control knob on the dash is pushed fully in.

(6) Pull the mixture control knob on the dash out approximately $\frac{5}{8}''$ without moving the carburetter jet heads away from contacting the lower face of the jet adjusting nuts.

(7) With the control in this position, adjust the fast idle adjusting screws, to give an engine fast idle speed of approximately 100 rpm at normal operating temperature.

JAGUAR XKE & MK10

These models are fitted with triple S.U. HD.8 type carburetors. The enrichment device for starting is in the form of an auxiliary carburetor attached to the front carburetor.

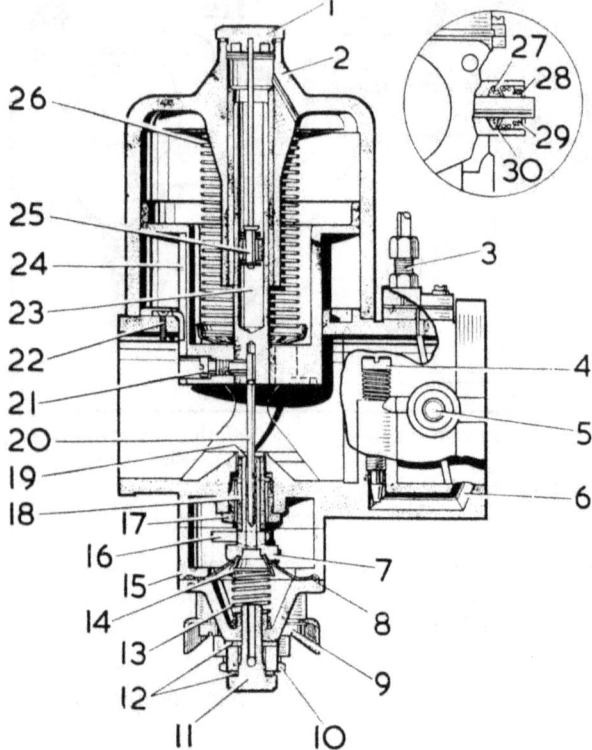

Fig. 1. Sectioned view of the HD.8 carburetter

1. Damper cap
2. Suction chamber
3. Union for vacuum advance/retard
4. Slow running volume screw
5. Throttle spindle
6. Slow run passage
7. Jet cup
8. Diaphragm
9. Float chamber securing screw
10. Banjo bolt
11. Banjo bolt
12. Fibre washers
13. Jet return spring
14. Return spring cup
15. Diaphragm casing
16. Actuating lever
17. Nut—jet bearing
18. Jet bearing
19. Jet
20. Needle
21. Needle retaining screw
22. Piston guide—retaining screw
23. Oil reservoir
24. Piston
25. Damper
26. Piston return spring
27. Throttle spindle gland
28. Shroud for spring
29. Spring
30. Washer

> As noted in the index, certain of the carburetor models discussed here are also fitted to other automobile makes. Some minor differences in mounting and linkage prevail, but all maintenance and adjustment data given here can be applied.

The HD type differs from the earlier type in that the jet glands are replaced by a flexible diaphragm, and the idling mixture is conducted along a passage way, in which is located a metering screw, instead of being controlled by a throttle disc.

The jet **19 (Fig. 1)**, which is fed through its lower end, is attached to a sythetic rubber diaphragm **8** by means of the jet cup **7** and jet return spring cup **14**, the center of the diaphragm being compressed between these two parts; at its outer edge it is held between the diaphragm casing **15** and the float chamber arm. The jet is controlled by the jet return spring **13** and the jet actuating lever **16**, the latter having an external adjusting screw which limits the upward travel of the jet and thus controls the mixture adjustment; screwing it in (clockwise) enriches the mixture, and unscrewing it weakens the mixture.

Throttle Spindle Glands

Provision is made for the use of throttle spindle glands consisting of the cork gland itself **27 (Fig. 1)**, a dished retaining washer **30**, a spring **29** and a shroud **28**. This assembly should not require servicing and can only be removed by dismantling the throttle spindle and disc.

Idling

The carburetor idles on the main jet and the mixture is conducted along the passage way **6 (Fig. 1)** connecting the choke space to the other side of the throttle disc.

The quantity of the mixture passing through the passage way and, therefore, the idling speed of the engine, is controlled by the "slow-run" valve **4**, the quality of relative richness of the mixture being determined by the jet adjusting screw. It follows that when idling, the throttle remains completely closed against the bore of the carburetor.

DATA

Type .... S.U. HD 8 (triple)   Jet needle type .... UM
Size .... 2" (5.08 cm.)   Jet size ... 0.125" (3.17 mm.)
Auxiliary starting carburetor—needle type 425/8

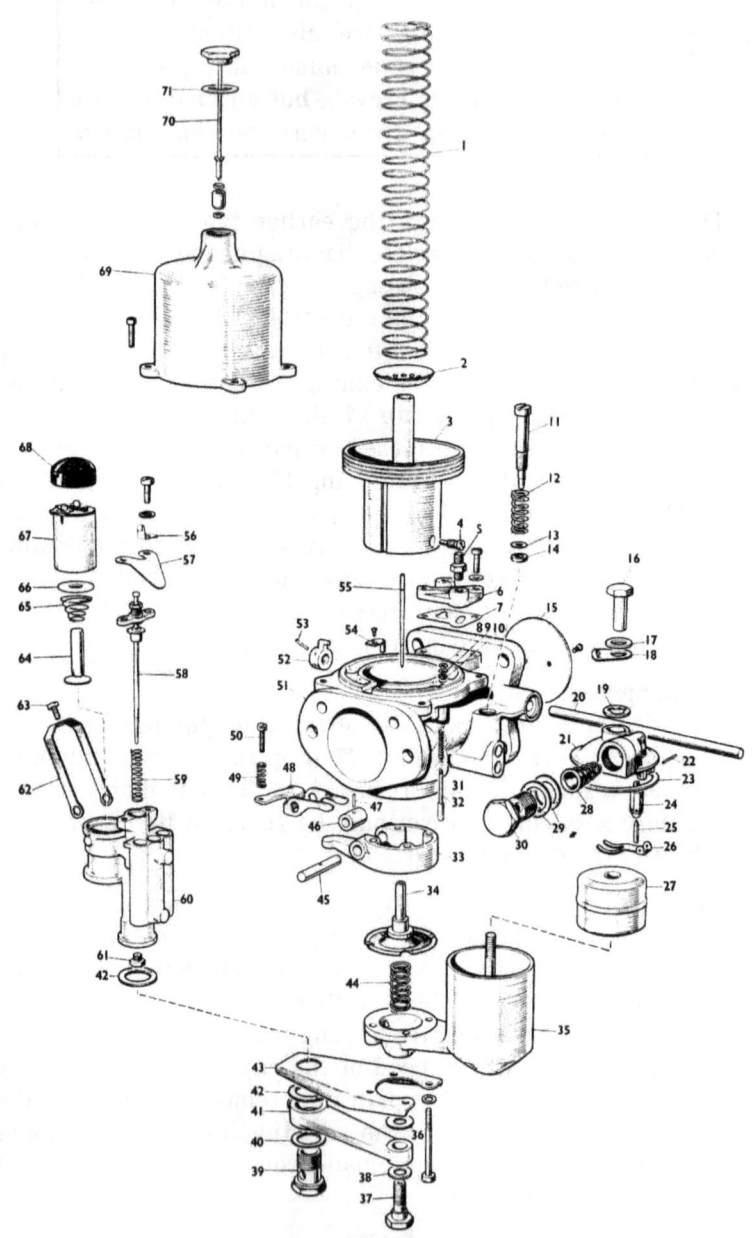

Fig. 2. Exploded view of the HD.8 carburetter and auxiliary starting carburetter

1. Spring
2. Skid washer
3. Piston
4. Retaining screw
5. Ignition union adaptor
6. Adaptor plate
7. Gasket
8. Spring washer
9. Washer
10. Nut
11. Slow running control screw
12. Spring
13. Brass washer
14. Neoprene washer
15. Throttle butterfly plate
16. Cap nut
17. Packing washer
18. Aluminium washer tag
19. Fibre serrated washer
20. Throttle spindle
21. Float chamber lid
22. Knurled pin
23. Gasket
24. Float needle seating
25. Float needle
26. Float needle lever
27. Float
28. Filter
29. Fibre washers
30. Banjo bolt
31. Spring
32. Piston lifting pin
33. Jet unit housing
34. Diaphragm
35. Float chamber
36. Fibre washer
37. Banjo bolt
38. Aluminium washer
39. Banjo bolt
40. Fibre washer
41. Connecting arm
42. Fibre washer
43. Bracket
44. Spring
45. Spindle
46. Distance piece
47. Locating pin
48. Lifting fork
49. Spring
50. Setscrew
51. Carburetter body
52. Throttle spindle stop
53. Shear pin
54. Piston guide
55. Needle
56. Spring clip
57. Dust shield
58. Auxiliary starter carburetter needle
59. Spring
60. Auxiliary starter carburetter body
61. Jet
62. Solenoid retaining clip
63. Pinch screw
64. Iron core disc valve
65. Conical spring
66. Washer
67. Solenoid
68. Solenoid cap
69. Suction chamber
70. Damper
71. Fibre washer

NOTE:

The jet needle type is stamped on the side or top face of the parallel portion of the needle. The auxiliary starting carburetor needle is stamped with the large number (eg. 425) on the shoulder of the needle, with the small number on the parallel portion of the needle.

ROUTINE MAINTENANCE

Warning: If it is desired to clean out the float chamber, do not use compressed air as this may cause rupture of the rubber jet diaphragm.

Every 2,500 Miles (4,000 Km.)

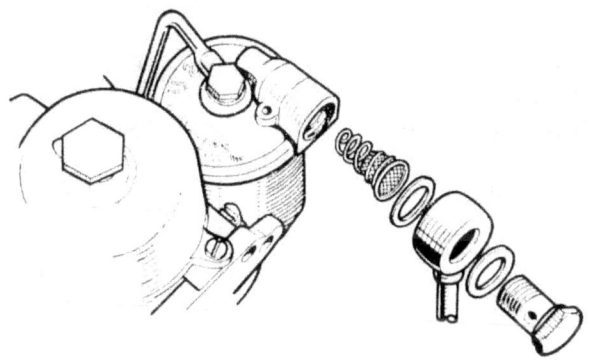

Fig. 4. Exploded view of the carburetter filter

Lubricate Carburetor Piston Damper

Each carburetor is fitted with a hydraulic piston damper which, unless periodically replenished with oil, will cause poor acceleration and spitting back through the carburetor on rapid opening of the throttle.

To replenish with oil, unscrew the cap on top of the suction chambers and lift out the damper valve which is attached to the cap. Fill the hollow piston spindle, which can be seen down inside the bore of the suction chamber, with S.A.E. 20 engine oil.

Checking Slow Running

The idling speed of the engine should be 500 r.p.m. when the engine is at its normal working temperature.

If adjustment is required turn the three slow running volume screws (see **Fig. 7**) **by exactly equal amounts** until the idling speed, observed on the revolution counter instrument, is correct.

Every 5,000 Miles (8,000 Km.)
Cleaning Carburetor Filters

Removal of the bolt securing the fuel pipe banjo union to each float chamber will expose the filters. Remove the filter and clean in gasoline, do not use a cloth as particles will stick to the gauze.

When refitting, insert the filter with the spring first and ensure that the fiber washers are replaced, one to each side of the banjo union.

1. Lid
2. Gauze filter
3. Cork washer
4. Glass bowl

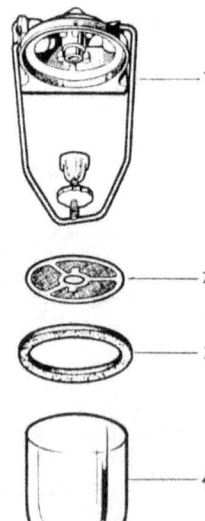

Fig. 5. Fuel feed line filter

CARBURETOR REMOVAL & REFITTING

Since rubber "O" rings are fitted between the carburetors and manifold flanges, it is of the utmost importance that no attempt should be made to remove the carburetors from the manifolds while in position in the car.

The necessity of making sure the "O" rings are securely placed in the annular grooves of the aluminum packing pieces **(Fig. 6)** can only be checked with the carburetors and manifolds off the engine. Therefore, to remove the carburetors, proceed as follows:
1. Remove the ground led from the battery.
2. Drain the radiator.
3. Remove the air clener flexible hose.
4. Disconnect the bretaher pipe situated between the front and middle carburetors.
5. Remove the six nuts and shakeproof washers retaining the air intake box. Withdraw the air intake box and collect the three joints fitted between the intake box and carburetor flanges. Remove the three banjo bolts and six fiber washers retaining the fuel pipe.
6. Remove the vacuum advance pipe from the front carburetor by unscrewing the union nut.
7. Disconnect the throttle rod at the rer end of the inlet manifold balance pipe. Disconnect the green/blue cable at the temperature transmiter unit.
8. Disconnect the green/black cable at the thermostat switch and the green/black, green cables at the auxiliary starter carburetor.
9. Disconnect the green/yellow cable at the anti-creep switch (if fitted). Slacken the clips and disconnect the top water hose and by-pass hoses from the inlet manifold water jacket. Slacken the clips at the rear of the inlet manifold water pipe and heater unit.
10. Disconnect the vacuum pipe from the base of the water valve.
11. Remove the nut at the base of the water valve and withdraw the water valve and heater hoses.
12. Slacken the clips and remove the two vacuum pipes from the tee-piece at the rear of the inlet manifold balance pipe.
13. Remove the setscrew retaining the float chamber drain pipes to the oil filter body.
14. Remove the nuts and spring washers securing the inlet manifolds to the cylinder head.
15. Detach the heater pipe clips and cable retaining clips on

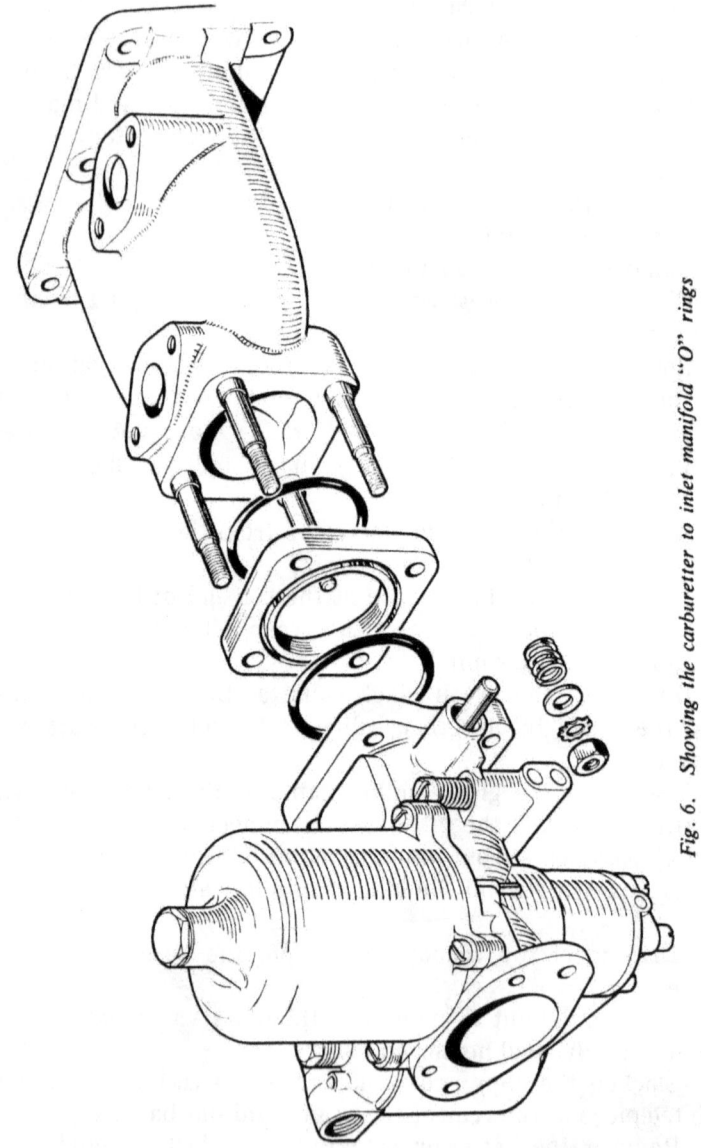

Fig. 6. Showing the carburetter to inlet manifold "O" rings

the bottom manifold studs.
16. Withdraw the manifolds and carburetors.
17. Disconnect the three butterfly return springs.
18. Disconnect the throttle links which are clipped to throttle spindle levers.
19. Unscrew the union retaining the auxiliary starter carburetor induction tract.
20. Remove the four self-locking nuts, washers and springs from each carburetor.
21. Remove the throttle spring brackets and anti-creep switch.
22. Remove the three carburetors and note carefully the position of the two rubber "O" rings and aluminum distance piece on each carburetor.

Refitting

Refitting is the reverse of the removal procedure, but note should be taken of the following points.

The "O" rings should be inspected for any signs of deterioration, that is, cuts, swelling or perishing of the rubber. The self-locking nuts should be screwed down until they meet the stud shoulder and stop turning. It should be possible to flex the carburetors up and down very slightly.

CLEANING THE SUCTION CHAMBER AND PISTON

This should be done at approximate intervals of every twelve months or if the carburetor is dismantled for any reason. After detaching, clean the main inside bore of the suction chamber and the two outside diameters of the piston with a rag moistened in fuel or thinners and then reassemble in a dry and clean condition with a few spots of thin oil on the piston rod only. Do NOT use metal polish to clean the suction chamber and piston.

CARBURETOR TUNING

Before tuning the carburetors, the spark plug gaps and contact breaker gaps should be checked and adjusted if necessary. The distributor centrifugal advance mechanism and vacuum advance operation should be checked and ignition timing set to 10° BTDC with the centrifugal advance mechanism in the static position. For final road test, adjustment of not more than six clicks of the micrometer adjustment at the distributor to either advance or retard is permitted. The ignition setting is important since if retarded or advanced too far the setting of the carburetors will be affected. As the needle size is determined during engine development, tuning of the carburetors is confined to the correct idling setting.

If after tuning the carburetors, the idling setting and engine performance is not satisfactory, it will be necessary to check the cylinder compressions and the valve clerances.

If an SU TAAL is available, tuning and synchronization are greatly simplified. If not, the following factory-advised method can be followed.

Tuning

Run the engine until it has attained its normal operating temperature.

Remove the air cleaner flexible hose. Disconnect the breather pipe situated between the front and middle carburetors. Remove the six nuts and shakeproof washers retaining the air intake box. Withdraw the air intake box and collect the three joints fitted between the intake box and carburetor flanges.

Slacken off the anti-creep throttle switch lever. Release the three pinch bolts securing the two piece throttle levers to the carburetor throttle spindles.

Taking one carburetor at a time, close each throttle butterfly valve fully by rotating the throttle spindle in a clockwise direction looking from the front; with the throttle held closed tighten the pinch bolt keeping the two piece throttle lever in the midway position (see **Fig. 8**).

Repeat for the other two carburetors, then operate the accelerator linkage and observe if all the throttles are opening simultaneously by noting the movement of the full throttle stops at the left-hand side of the throttle spindles.

NOTE:

On initial movement of the accelerator linkage there should be a limited amount of lost motion at the throttle spindles; this ensures that all the throttle butterfly valves can return to the fully closed position. Re-position the anti-creep throttle switch lever so that the switch is depressed when the throttles are closed.

Screw down the slow running volume screws (**A, Fig. 7**) on to their settings and then unscrew two full turns. Remove the piston and suction chambers, ensure that the needles are correctly located in the piston, that is, with the lower edge of the groove flush wtih the base of the piston (see **Fig. 9**). Unscrew the mixture adjusting screws **B** until each jet is flush with the bridge of its carburetor. Replace the pistons and suction chambers and check that each piston falls freely on to the bridge of its carburetor (by means of the piston lifting pin). Turn down the mixture adjusting screws 2½ turns.

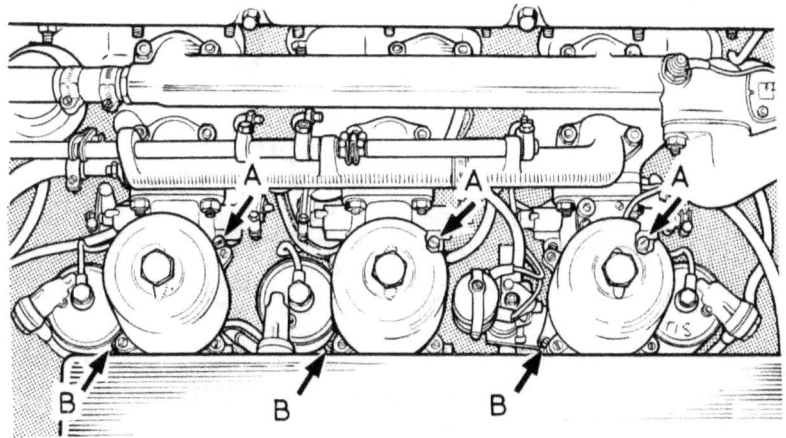

Fig. 7. "A"—Slow running volume screw "B"—Mixture adjusting screw

Restart the engine and adjust to the desired idling speed of 500 r.p.m. by moving each slow running screw an equal amount. By listening to the hiss in the intakes, adjust the slow running screws until the intensity of the hiss is similar on all intakes. This will synchronize the mixture flow of the three carburetors.

When this is satisfactory the mixture should be adjusted by screwing all the mixture adjusting screws up (weaker) or down (richer) by the same amount until the fastest idling speed is obtained consistent with even firing.

As the mixture is adjusted, the engine will probably run faster and it may therefore be necessary to screw down the slow running volume screws in order to reduce the speed.

Now check the mixture strength by lifting the piston of the front carburetor by approximately $\frac{1}{32}''$ (.8 mm) when, if:

a) the engine speed increases and **continues to run faster,** this indicates that the mixture is too rich.

b) the engine speed immediately decreases, this indicates that the mixture is too weak.

c) the engine speed **momentarily** increases very slightly, this indicates that the mixture is correct.

Repeat the operation at the remaining two carburetors and after adjustment recheck the front carburetor since the carburetors are interdependent.

When the mixture is correct, the exhaust note should be regular and even. If it is irregular, with a splashy type of misfire and colorless exhaust, the mixture is too weak. If there is a regular or rythmical type of misfire in the exhaust beat together with a blackish exhaust, then the mixture is too rich.

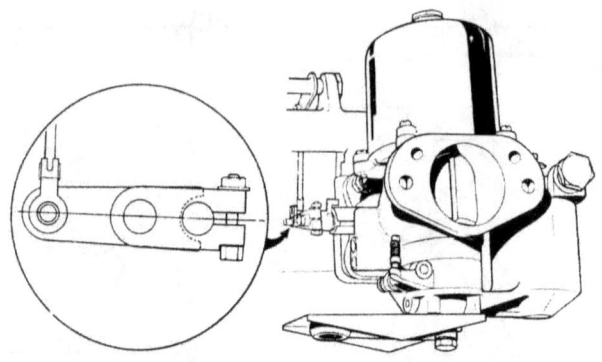

Fig. 8. Two piece throttle lever. Inset shows it in the midway position

Float Chamber Fuel Level

When the fuel level setting is correct a $\frac{7}{16}''$ (11.1 mm.) test bar will just slide between the lid face and the inside curve of the float lever fork when the needle valve is in the "shut-off" position (see **Fig. 11**).

If the float lever fails to conform with this check figure, it must be carefully bent at the start of the fork section, in the necessary direction, for correction. Take care to keep both prongs of the fork level with each other and maintain the straight portion of the lever dead flat.

It is not advisable to alter the fuel level unless there is trouble with flooding; although too high a level can cause slow flooding, particularly when a car is left ticking over on a steep drive. It should be remembered that flooding can also be caused by grit in the fuel jamming open the needle valve, undue friction in

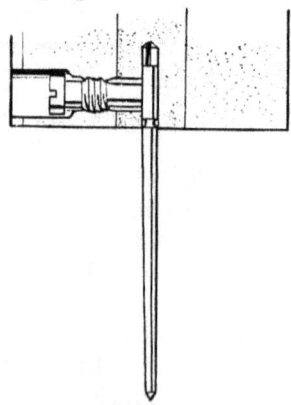

Fig. 9. Positioning the jet needle with the lower edge of the groove flush with the base of the piston

the float gear, excessive engine vibration, or a porous float.

CENTERING THE JET

Warning: Take care not to bend the jet needle when carrying out this operation.

Remove the carburetor from the engine as described previously.

Remove the four setscrews securing the float chamber to the carburetor body. Remove the float chamber, jet housing and jet. Remove the hydraulic damper.

Slacken the jet locking nut approximately half a turn. Replace the jet and diaphragm assembly.

The jet is correctly centered when the piston falls freely and hits the jet "bridge" with a metallic click. To center the jet, push the jet and diaphragm assembly as high as possible with the hand and with a pencil or rod gently press the piston down on the jet bridge; centralization will be facilitated if the side of the carburetor body is tapped lightly. Tighten the jet locking nut.

The actual centering must be carried out with the setscrew holes in the jet diaphragm and carburetor in alignment. After tightening the jet locking nut, the jet diaphragm must be kept in the same position relative to the carburetor body; the simplest way to do this is to mark one of the corresponding jet diaphragm and carburetor body setscrew holes with a soft pencil. Failure to do this may cause the centralization to be upset.

Fig. 10. The carburetter piston lifting pin; the first part of the movement is spring loaded free travel

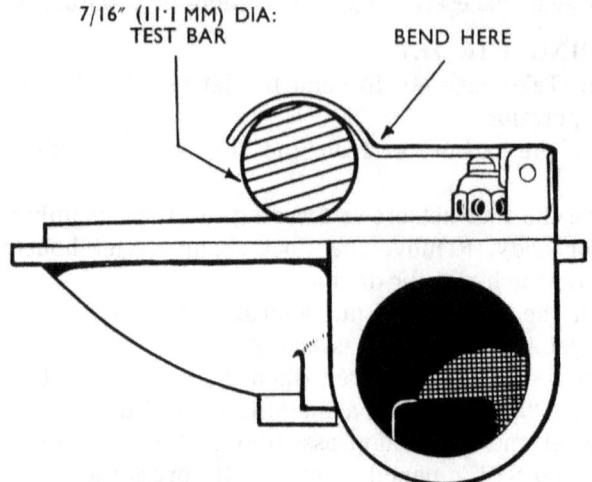

Fig. 11. Checking the float lever setting, which controls the fuel level in the float chamber

Check that the centralization is correct by noting if there is any difference in the sound of the piston hitting the jet bridge with the jet in its highest and lowest positions. If there is any difference in the sound, the procedure for centralizing the jet will have to be repeated.

If difficulty in centering the jet is encountered after carrying out the above procedure, the jet needle can be lowered slightly in the piston to make the centralizing effect more positive. The needle must, however, be restored to the normal position when checking the centralization.

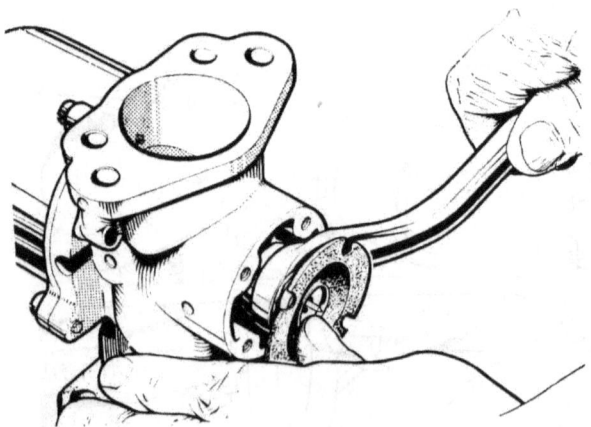

Fig. 12. Centring the jet

THE AUXILIARY STARTING CARBURETOR
Description

The enrichment apparatus for starting is, in effect, an auxiliary carbureting system. The main body casting (**1, Fig. 13**) containing a solenoid-operated valve and fuel metering system is a separate unit attached by means of a ducted mounting arm to the base of the front carburetor.

The auxiliary carburetor forms, therefore, a separate unit additional to the normal float chamber retained by the hollow cross-drilled bolt.

Fuel is supplied to the base of the jet **9**, which is obstructed to a greater or lesser degree by the tapered slidable needle **10**.

When the device is in action air is drawn from atmosphere

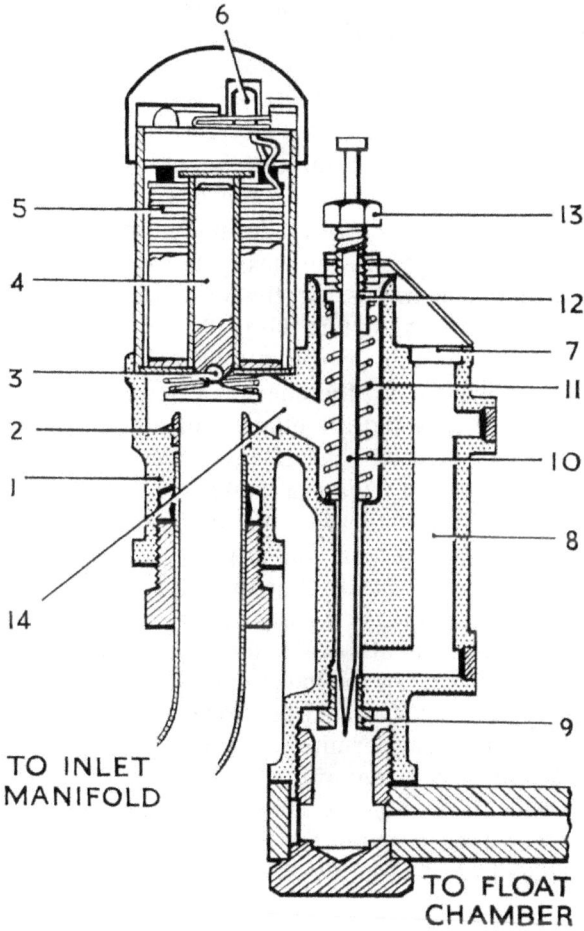

Fig. 13. Sectioned view of the auxiliary starting carburetter

through the air intake 7 and thence through the passage 8, being carburetted with fuel as it passes the jet 9. The mixture is thence carried upwards past the shank of the needle 10 through the passage 14 and so past the aperture provided between the valve 3 and its seating 2. From here it passes directly to the inlet manifold through an external feed pipe.

The device is brought into action by energizing the winding of the solenoid 5 from the terminals 6. The centrally located iron core 4 is thus raised magnetically, carrying with it the ball-jointed disc valve 3 against the load of the small conical spring and thus uncovering the aperture provided by the seating 2.

Considering the function of the slidable needle 10, it will be seen that this is loaded upwards in its open position by means of the light compression spring 11 which abuts against a disc 12 attached to the shank of the needle. The needle continues upwards through the vertical adjustable stop 13 and finally terminates in an enlarged head.

Vacuum within the space surrounding the spring 11 is directly derived from that prevailing in the induction tract, and this exerts a downward force upon the disc 12, which is provided with an adequate clearance for its surrounding bore. This tends to overcome the load of the spring 11 and to move the needle downwards, thus increasing the obstruction afforded by the tapered section which enters the jet 9.

The purpose of this device is to provide two widely different degrees of enrichment, the one corresponding to idling or light cruising conditions and the other to conditions of open throttle or full-power operation. In effect, under the former conditions the high induction vacuum prevailing will cause the disc 12 to be drawn downwards, drawing the tapered needle into the jet 9, while under the latter, the lower vacuum existing in the induction tract will permit the collar to maintain its upward position wih the needle withdrawn from the jet.

The tuning elements concerned in this device are the size and degree of taper of the lower end of the needle 10, the diameter of the disc 12, the load provided by the spring 11 and the degree of movement permitted to the needle assembly, as determined by the adjustment of the stop 13.

The solenoid 5 is energized by means of a thermostatically operated switch housed in the inlet manifold water jacket. This is arranged below about 30-35°C. (86-95°F.) .

Adjustment

The engine must be at its normal running temperature before any attempt is made to tune the auxiliary enrichment device.

As it can generally be assumed that the tapered form of the needle 10, the strength of the spring 11, and the diameter of the disc 12 have already been appropriately chosen, tuning is generally confined to the adjustment of the stop screw 13. It will be appreciated that the main purpose of this adjustment is to limit the downward movement of the needle, the head of which abuts against the upper surface of the stop screw at the lower extremity of its travel. The final downward movement of this needle determines, as has been described, the degree of enrichment provided under idling conditions with the auxiliary carburetor in operation. An appropriate guide to its correct adjustment in this respect is provided by energizing the solenoid when the engine has already attained its normal temperature. The stop screw 13 should then be so adjusted that the mixture is distinctly although not excessively rich, that is to say, until the exhaust gases are seen to be discernibly black in color, but just short of the point where the engine commences to run with noticeable irregularity.

Anti-clockwise rotation of the stop screw will, of course, raise the needle under these conditions and increase the mixture strength, while rotation in the opposite direction will have the opposite effect. In order to energize the solenoid under conditions when the thermostatic switch will normally have broken the circuit, it is merely necessary to short-circuit the terminal of the thermostatic switch directly to ground wih a screwdriver and flick open the throttles when the starting device will be heard to come into operation with a pronounced hissing noise.

Thermostatic Switch—Removal

The thermostatic switch which controls the operation of the auxiliary starting carburetor is situated at the front end of the inlet manifold water jacket.

Remove the electrical cable from the switch by removing the chrome plated domed nut.

If the radiator filler cap is securely tightened no appreciable amount of water will escape when the auxiliary starting carburetor switch is removed. Alternatively, a small amount of water can be drained from the radiator.

Remove the three securing setscrews and washers and withdraw the switch and the cork gasket.

Refitting

Refitting is the reverse of the removal procedure. A new cork gasket must be fitted when the switch is replaced. If any water has been drained from the radiator or has escaped during

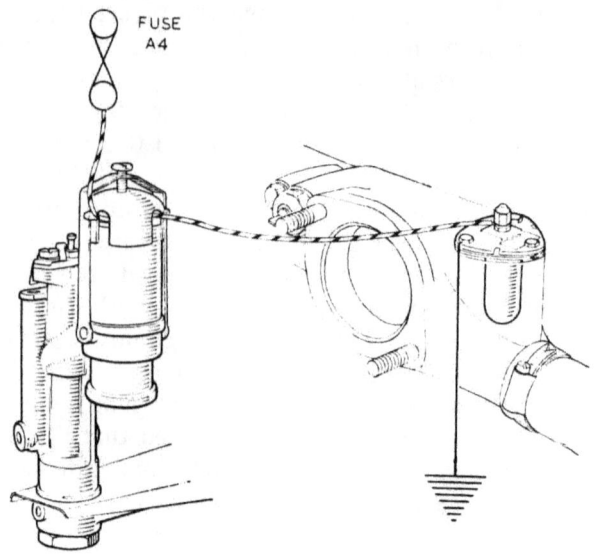

Fig. 15. Wiring circuit for the auxiliary starter carburetter to the thermostatic switch

the removal of the switch, the radiator should be topped up to the correct level.

ACCELERATOR LINKAGE ADJUSTMENT—MK 10 (R.H. Drive)

NOTE:

It is important to obtain the correct angle of the accelerator lever brackets for satisfactory operation of the accelerator controls.

Setting the complete accelerator linkage

1. Remove the connecting link (**A, Fig. 16**) (spring control rod on automatic transmission models).
2. Fit a 5¾" (14-60 cm) template between the accelerator pedal and the toe board.
3. Slacken off the pinch bolt **B** of the lever **C** and fit a 1⅝" (4.12 m) template between the bell crank lever **C** ball end and the outer diameter of the kick down cross shaft **D**. Lock up the pinch bolt on the accelerator cross shaft **B**.
4. To reset the slow motion link **E**, ensure that the carburetor throttle butterflies are shut. If necessary, this can be obtained by slackening off the pinch bolts on all the butterfly levers and adjusting the slow running stop eccentric to give ¹⁄₁₆" (1.58 mm) "offset" as shown in **Fig. 16**. Re-tighten the butterfly levers to the desired position; ensuring that a minimum of free play exists

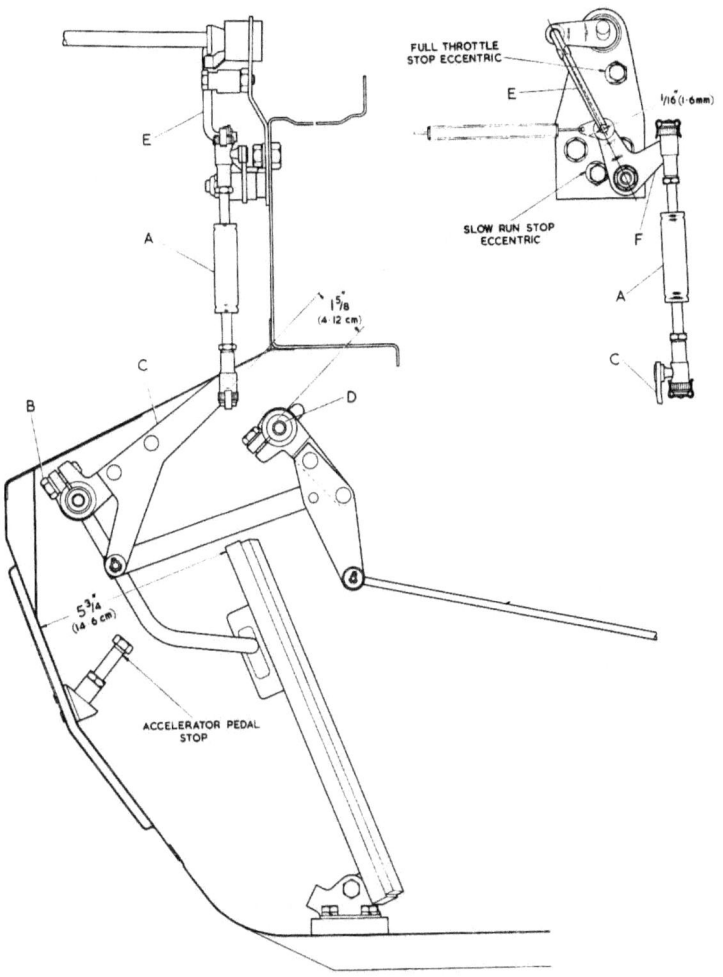

Fig. 16. Accelerator linkage—Right-hand drive

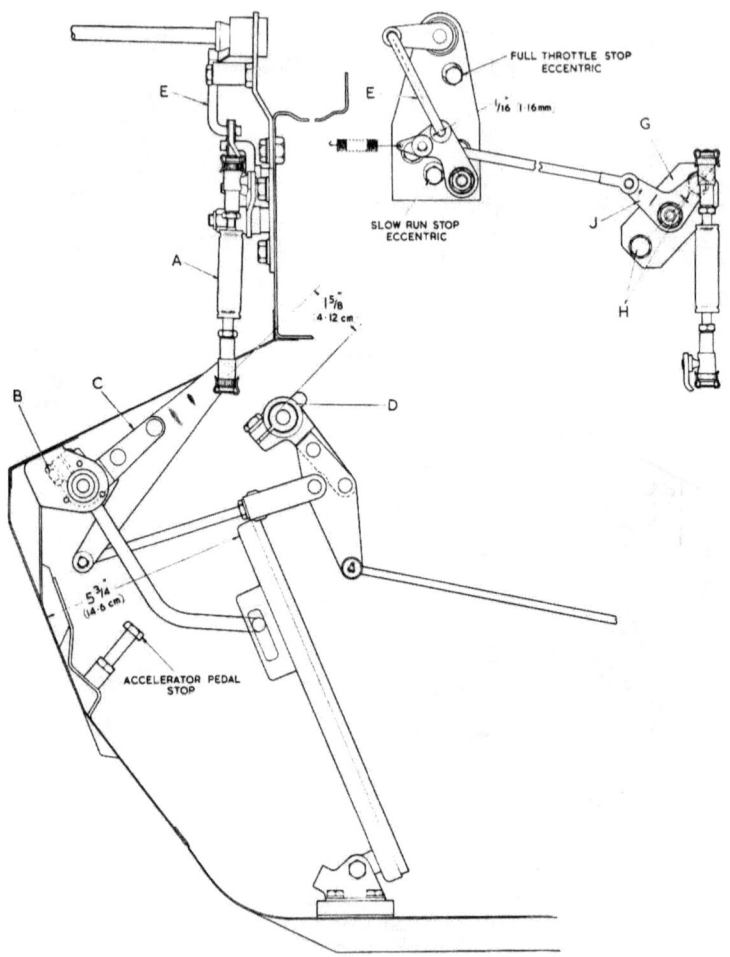

Fig. 17. *Accelerator linkage—Left-hand drive*

between the butterfly spindles and levers.

5. On automatic transmission models with the accelerator template still in position, adjust the kick down spring control rod **A** in length until it will fit the ball joints of levers **C** and **F**. DO NOT forget to tighten the spring control rod lock nuts.

6. Remove the accelerator pedal to toeboard template. Depress the accelerator pedal to the full throttle position; do NOT operate the linkage by hand to obtain full throttle. Adjust the full throttle stop eccentric until it is just touching the slow motion link.

ACCELERATOR LINKAGE ADJUSTMENT—MK 10 (L.H. Drive)

Proceed as for R.H. Drive in paragraphs 1, 2, 3 and 4.

5. Adjust the slave bell crank fulcrum bracket (**G, Fig. 17**) on the left-hand bulkhead by slackening off the two mounting setscrews **H**. Position the bracket so that the slave bell crank **J** is immediately in front of the fulcrum bracket upper setscrew **H**.

6. Proceed as for R.H. Drive in paragraphs 5 and 6.

NOTES

VOLVO

The make and model carburetor used on Volvos depends upon the engine type designation. B14 engines use twin S.U. H2 carburetors. B16A and B16D engines use a single Zenith 34 VN carburetor. Engines with a B16B designation use twin S.U. H4 carburetors. B18A powered units use a single Zenith 36 VN carburetor and Volvos with engines of B18B and B18D designations use twin S.U. HS6 carburetors.

CARBURETORS, SU H-2, H-4

Both the carburetors are fitted with a rapid idling device. The front carburetor in each pair is not fitted directly with this device but receives the same impulse through the shaft connecting the carburetors together.

There is an equalizer tube between both the inlet manifolds which are very short. There is only one jet in each of the carburetors. Fuel flow is varied by a tapered needle which is guided by a plunger in the carburetor, this plunger being influenced by

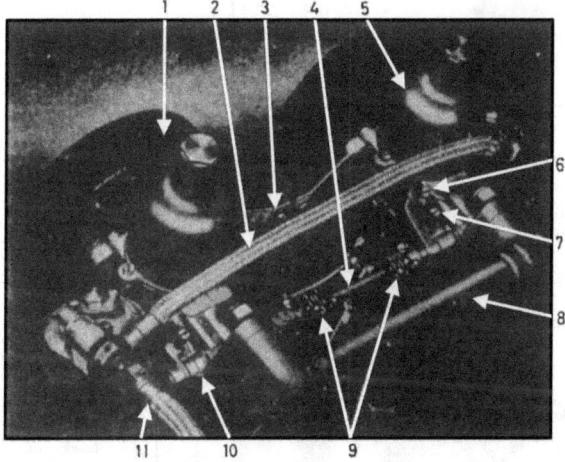

Fig. 15. SU carburetors (B 14 A and B 16 B engines).

1. Forward carburetor
2. Fuel pipe between carburetors
3. Retainer for controls
4. Shaft between carburetors
5. Rear carburetor
6. Rapid idling adjuster screw
7. Idling adjuster screw
8. Equalizer tube
9. Couplings
10. Idling adjuster screw
11. Fuel line from pump

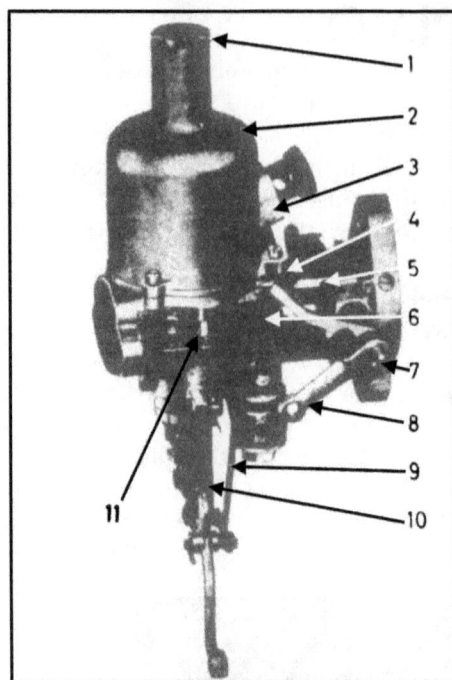

1. Nut for damping plunger (also for oil filling)
2. Suction chamber
3. Float bowl cover
4. Rapid idling adjuster screw
5. Idling adjuster screw
6. Cam plate
7. Throttle shaft
8. Throttle shaft lever
9. Link rod
10. Link
11. Lift pin for piston

Fig. 16. Rear SU carburetor from control side.

1. Suction chamber
2. Air channel
3. Piston
4. Seal washer
5. Lock nut
6. Spring
7. Lever
8. Adjuster nut
9. Lower part of jet
10. Spring
11. Float bowl

Fig. 17. Rear SU carburetor from float bowl side.

the degree of partial vacuum in the carburetor barrel. There is no choke in the normal sense of the term. Instead there is a cold starting device which, when engaged, gives a richer fuel/air mixture by depressing the jet whereupon the fuel flow area increases.

The function of the carburetor can be divided into the following groups:
1. Float system
2. Running
3. Cold starting
4. Rapid idling
5. Idling

1. **Float system.**

The fuel flow is controled by the float system so that the correct fuel level is obtained in the carburetor.

The float system consists of a float bowl (6) which is flexibly attached to the carburetor housing through the medium of rubber gaskets, as well as a float (5), cover (1) and the flexibly attached lever (4) together with the needle valve (3) which is attached to the cover. There is a strainer (2) with a spring in the cover. The float is guided by a center bolt in the float bowl.

When fuel is forced by the pump to the float bowl, it first passes through the strainer which removes all impurities. When the fuel level rises, the float is lifted upwards and when the fuel level has reached the height, the needle is pushed up by the lever so that the flow of fuel is stopped. When the level sinks, the valve opens again and more fuel flows in.

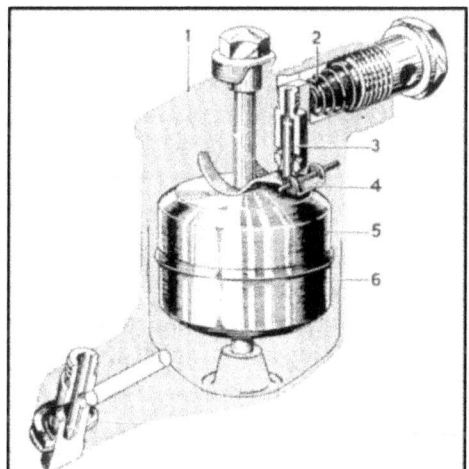

1. Float bowl cover
2. Strainer
3. Needle valve
4. Lever
5. Float
6. Float bowl

Fig. 18. Float system.

2. Running

The amount of fuel/air mixture which flows to the engine is regulated with the aid of the butterfly throttle (6) in the carburetor housing (7). The housing is in the shape of a channel but is also a body on which the various parts of the carburetor are assembled.

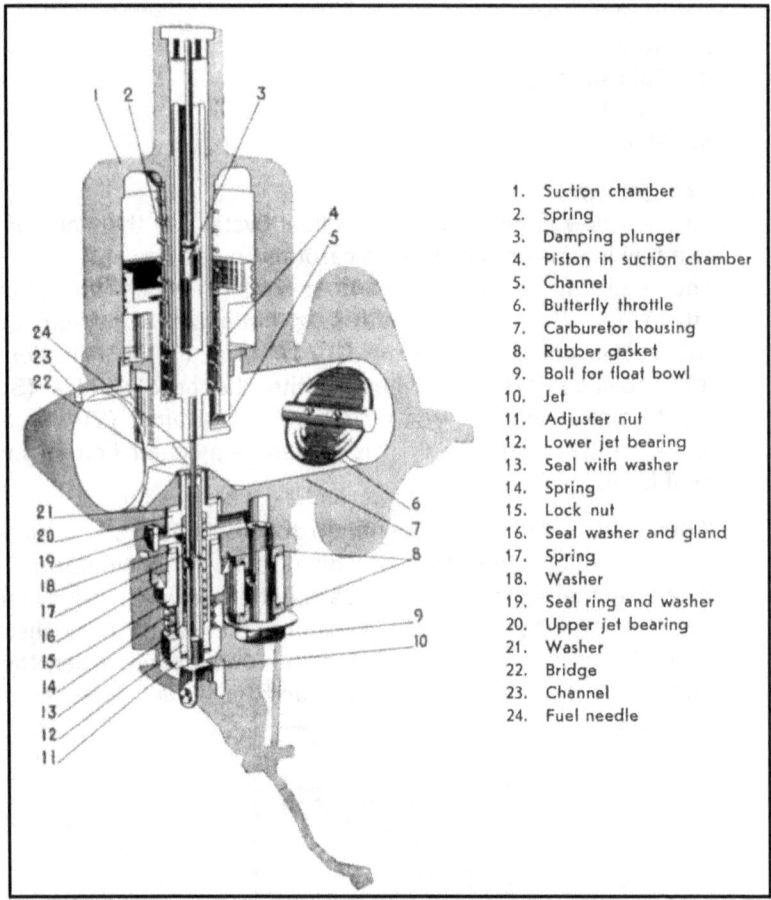

1. Suction chamber
2. Spring
3. Damping plunger
4. Piston in suction chamber
5. Channel
6. Butterfly throttle
7. Carburetor housing
8. Rubber gasket
9. Bolt for float bowl
10. Jet
11. Adjuster nut
12. Lower jet bearing
13. Seal with washer
14. Spring
15. Lock nut
16. Seal washer and gland
17. Spring
18. Washer
19. Seal ring and washer
20. Upper jet bearing
21. Washer
22. Bridge
23. Channel
24. Fuel needle

Fig. 19. Carburetor, operating position.

Above the jet (10) which is fitted from below, the channel narrows due to the projection known as the bridge (22) and the piston (4) which is situated above the bridge. The air flow speed increases when it passes through this restriction whereby the fuel is picked up more easily.

Opposite the bridge on the top of the carburetor, there is a suction chamber (1) with the piston (4). There is a tapered needle (24) attached to the lower section of the piston.

The piston is guided by a centrally located spindle which runs in the center part of the suction chamber where there is a bushing. The upper part of the piston is precision fitted into the suction chamber. The lower section functions as a shutter and restricts the cross-sectional area of the main air passage above the jet as the piston moves downwards. The piston, under the influence of its own weight and assisted by the spring (2) always shows a tendency to assume its lowest position. When the piston is in its lowest position it rests against the bridge by means of the pin fitted in it.

When the engine is running and the butterfly throttle opening increases, the degree of vacuum in the space between the bridge and the throttle increases and then the cavity above the piston is connected through a little channel (5) to the above-mentioned cavity and the piston moves upwards. The space below the upper section of the piston is connected to the outer air by means of a channel (23). (There are two channels on B 16 B carburetors).

When the piston rises, the carburetor channel cross-section above the jet is enlarged and an additional quantity of air is permitted to pass through. Since the fuel needle is attached to the piston, it also moves upwards and the effect of opening between the fuel needle and the jet is enlarged. A quantity of fuel corresponding to the larger quantity of air is then sucked in. The amount of fuel is regulated partly by the piston (fuel needle) position and partly by the air flow speed.

The jet is fed with fuel from the space in the carburetor housing at the float bowl connection through the hole in the jet walls.

The position of the piston will be stable for any given air flow through the carburetor. The degree of this air flow is determined by the degree of throttle opening as well as the speed of the engine and the loading on the engine. Every tendency on the part of the piston to move downwards will be accompanied by a reduction of the flow area between the bridge and the under side of the piston with the consequent increase of the degree of partial vacuum between the piston and the throttle. This immediately results in an increase in the partial vacuum in the upper part of the suction chamber. The piston will then be raised so much that balance is once more restored. There is a damping device in the recess in the piston spindle to prevent the piston from coming into any pendular motion or moving excessively rapidly. This device consists of a damping plunger (3) attached to the rod. The hollow interior of the spindle contains a quantity of light engine oil. The retarding effect of this damping device on rapid movement of the piston prevents the engine from stalling due to an excessively lean fuel/air mixture when the accelerator pedal is depressed rapidly.

Opposite the throttle (rear carburetor) there is a connection for the pipeline to the vacuum regulator on the distributor.

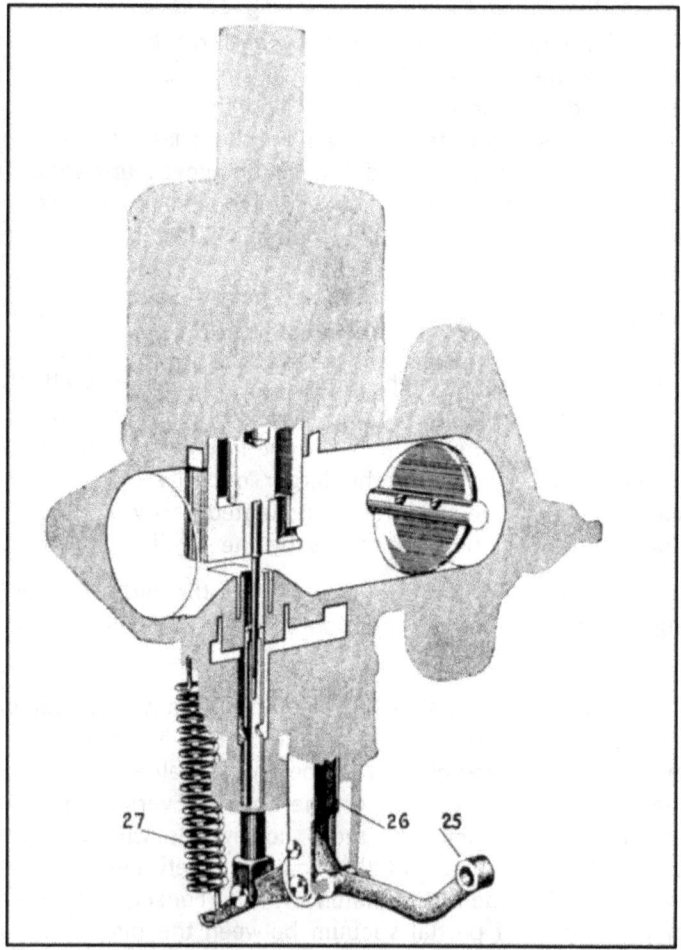

Fig. 20. Carburetor, cold start.

25. Lever
26. Link
27. Spring

3. **Cold Starting**
   In order to enrich the fuel/air mixture when starting a cold engine, there is a carburetor device by means of which the jet can be lowered. When the jet is lowered there will be a wider flow area for the fuel since the needle in the jet is tapered. There is no choke shutter on the carburetors. The jet, the lower part of which is yoke formed, is not fitted directly in the carburetor housing but is carried in two bearings (12 and 20) so that it can move up and down. When the lock nut (15) is loosened the jet can also be moved laterally (for centralizing). The upper bearing has a flange which with the aid of a washer (21), seals against the recess in the carburetor housing, the lower bearing flange sealing with the help of a washer (18) against the top of the lock nut. The lock nut seals against the carburetor housing by means of a washer and a gland (16). Inside the bearings there is a spring (17) exerting pressure against two washers with sealing glands (13 and 19) which prevent any leakage of fuel at the jet. When a cold engine is being started the outer end of the lever (25) is pulled upwards by means of a control system, the movement being transmitted to the link (26) so that the jet, which is connected to the inner end of the lever, is pulled downwards. This movement is limited by means of a projection on the lever and return to the normal position is taken care of by the return spring (27) when the control is pushed in. At the same time as this lever is operated, the throttle is opened slightly by means of the rapid idling device described below.

4. **Rapid Idling**
   When the rapid idling device is operated, a larger throttle opening is obtained than is usual during normal idling and this is used during the engine warming-up period in order to obtain a somewhat higher idling speed. See fig. 21.

   This device, which is connected to the cold starting device, consists of a link rod (31) connected to the lower lever which influences a cam-shaped plate (30) attached to the carburetor housing. There is an adjuster screw which contacts this plate when the rapid idling device is in operation. This screw is attached to the throttle lever (28). When the lower, outer end of the lever is lifted, the cam-shaped plate is turned by which the throttle is opened slightly. (The end of the lever can be lifted slightly before the jet is influenced depending upon the large clearance in the lever hole on the link).

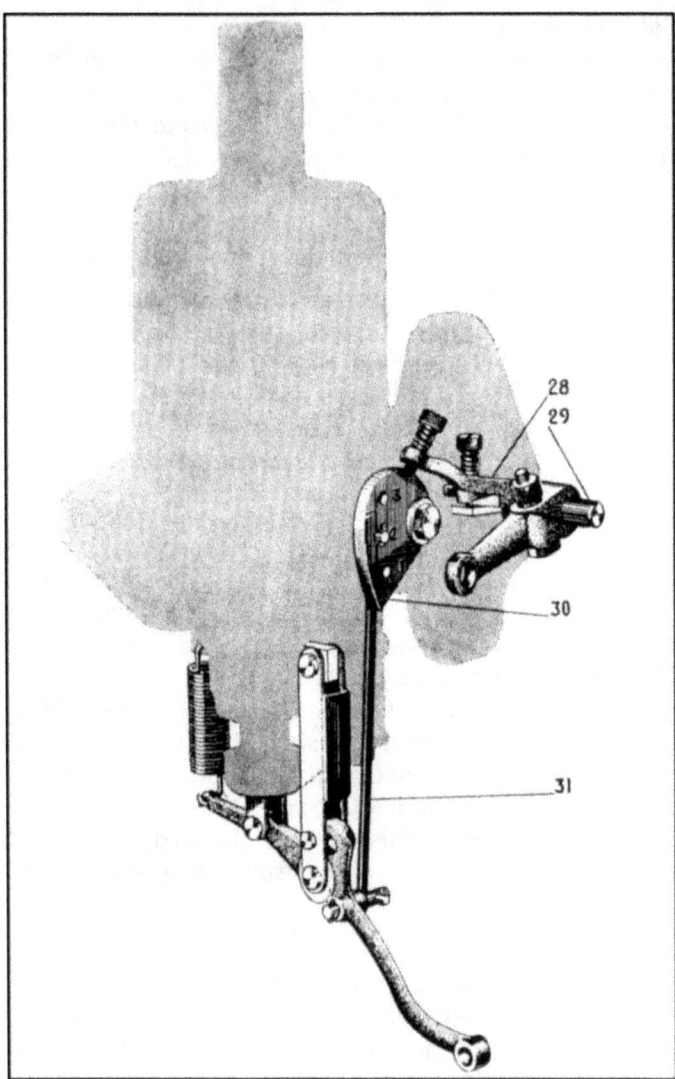

Fig. 21. Carburetor, rapid idling.
- 28. Lever for throttle
- 29. Throttle shaft
- 30. Cam plate
- 31. Link rod

5. **Idling**

When the engine is idling the carburetor piston is in its lowest position and rests on the bridge at the jet on a pin. The small opening which remains between the bridge and the piston allows the required amount of air to pass for idling without there being a sufficiently great degree of partial vacuum to raise the piston.

The amount of fuel required for idling is very small and the tapered needle almost entirely fills the jet opening.

The jet is pressed upwards by the spring (10 figure 17) so that the lower part of the jet is supported against the adjuster nut (8) which is locked in position by means of a spring (6). This nut is used to set the amount of fuel passing through since the fuel needle is tapered.

If the nut is screwed upwards a leaner fuel/air mixture is obtained and if the nut is screwed downwards, the mixture will be richer.

The relationship between fuel and air is set at idling for the complete speed range.

B 16 B

Type	Horizontal (2)
Make and designation	SU H4
Number of carburetters	2
Size (air intake diameter)	38 mm ($1^{1/2}''$)
Fuel control jet, designation	AUC 2112
Fuel needle, designation	GT
when using intake silencer air cleaner	GW
Rapid idling, setting of rod in cam-shaped lever	Position 2
Idling speed	500—700 r.p.m.

SU CARBURETOR TYPE HS-6

The operating principle of this carburetor (found on the B 18 B and B 18 D engines) is identical to that described above. Except for variations in the design of the float system and in the cold starting enrichment method, they can be treated in the same fashion.

Type	Horizontal, twin
Make and type	SU—HS 6
No. of carburetters	2
Size (air intake)	44.5 mm ($1^{3/4}''$)
Fuel needle, designation	K . A
Idling speed	500—700 r.p.m.
Oil for damping cylinders	SAE 20 engine oil

CARBURETORS, SU H-2, H-4
Disassembly

1. Blow the carburetors clean externally.
2. Loosen and remove the air cleaners and the control retainer with the control rod between them.
3. Remove the fuel line connections and the vacuum line connections (to the distributor).
4. Loosen the nuts on the connections on the shaft between the carburetors. Move up the connections on the shaft. Loosen the throttle controls. Remove the carburetors.

Disassembly and cleaning
Float Bowl
1. Loosen the float bowl from the carburetor housing.
2. Remove the nut on the float bowl cover. Remove the cap and lift out the float.
3. Remove the float arm by pulling out the pin upon which it pivots.
4. Loosen the needle valve in the cover and the hollow bolt and strainer.

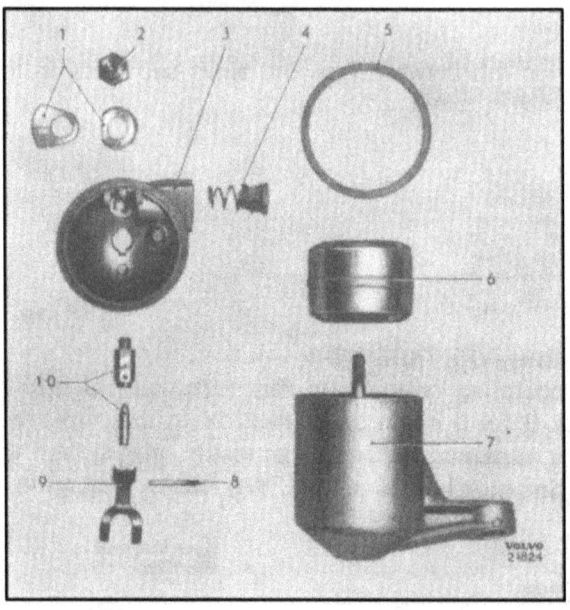

Fig. 84. Float-bowl assembly (SU).

1. Washers
2. Nut
3. Float bowl cover
4. Strainer and spring
5. Gasket
6. Float
7. Float bowl
8. Pin
9. Lever
10. Needle valve

Jet unit
1. Remove the return spring for the jet lever and the link rod between the lever and the cam-shaped plate.
2. Remove the bolt for the jet head and the upper bolt for the link and then remove the lever.
3. Remove the lock nut and take out the jet bearings with the spring and gland. Pull out the jet. Screw off the adjuster nut and remove its spring.

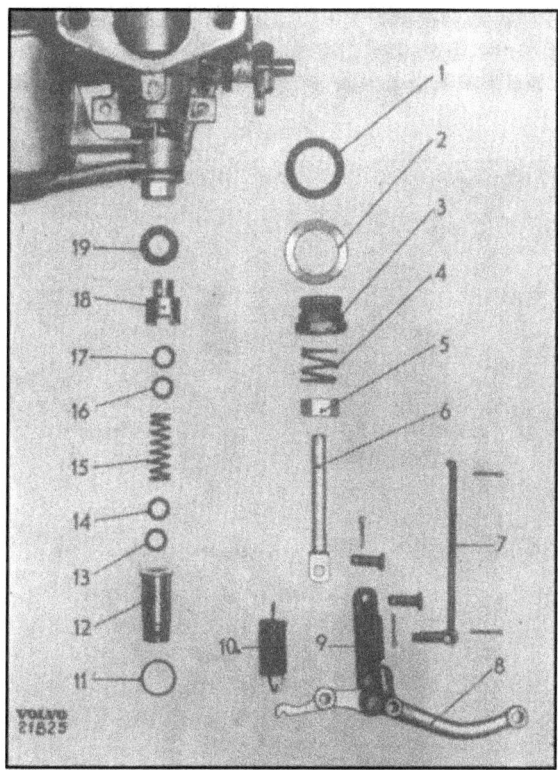

Fig. 85. Jet unit disassembled (SU).

1. Washer
2. Seal washer
3. Lock nut
4. Spring
5. Adjuster nut
6. Jet
7. Link rod
8. Lever
9. Link
10. Spring
11. Washer
12. Lower jet bearing
13. Seal ring
14. Washer
15. Spring
16. Washer
17. Seal ring
18. Upper jet bearing
19. Washer

Suction chamber with piston and fuel needle

The suction chamber and the piston are matched as units and if one of these is replaced then the other must be replaced at the same time. The suction chamber has three attaching screws which are staggered to ensure that it is fitted the right way. B 14 carburetors have two screws. Do not turn suction chamber.
1. Remove the damper from the suction chamber.
2. Loosen the screws on the suction chamber and lift out.

3. Lift up the spring and the piston. Take care to ensure that the needle is not damaged (bent).
4. Screw out the lock screw on the fuel needle and pull it out.

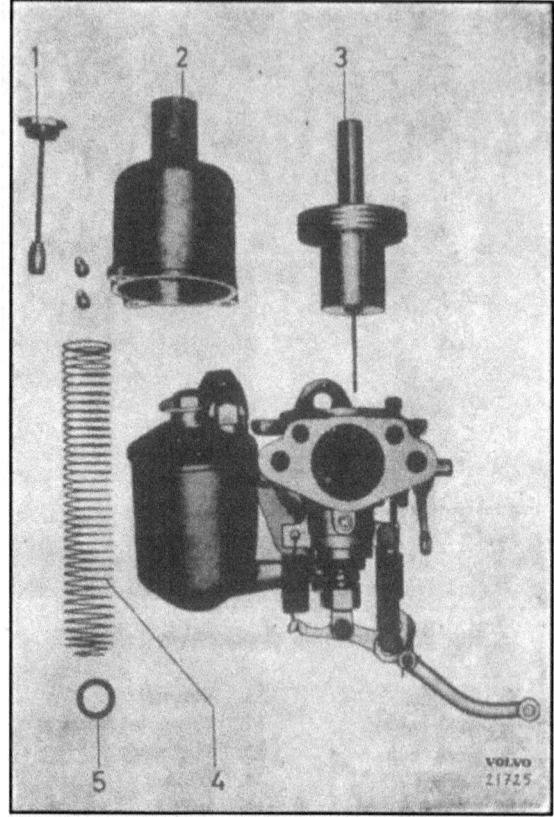

Fig. 86. Suction chamber disassembled (SU).

1. Damping plunger
2. Suction chamber
3. Piston
4. Spring
5. Washer

Cleaning
After disassembly, all parts should be cleaned in kerosene and then be blown clean with compressed air.

Assembly and fitting
Assembly and refitting on the engine is carried out in reverse to that used when disassembling and removing.

Before assembling, check that all gaskets and sealing glands are free from damage. Replace these if necessary. Make sure that all other parts are neither damaged or worn.

Neither the suction chamber nor the piston may be filed or rubbed with emery paper since this will change the fit and this has been very carefully calculated so that the carburetor will function properly. Any small unevenness can, however, be carefully rubbed away.

When attaching the needle in the piston it is very important to ensure that the needle assumes the right position as far as gap is concerned. See under the heading "Replacement of fuel needle." The piston in the suction chamber is grooved and a guide projection in the carburetor housing fits into this groove. Lubricate the piston spindle lightly with thin engine oil before reassembling.

When the jet is fitted, it must be centralized before it is tightened. Otherwise the needle can jam or, under unfavorable circumstances, become damaged. See under the heading "Centralizing the jet."

Add oil (engine oil SAE 5 W) to the damping cylinders after reassembling the carburetors. The air holes in the air cleaners must not be blocked.

Fig. 87. Jet unit assembled (SU).

1. Jet and associated parts

Checking the fuel level

The fuel level can be checked indirectly after removing the float bowl cover.
1. Loosen the fuel line and remove the float bowl cover.
2. Turn the float bowl cover upside down.
3. Measure the distance from the float bowl cover to the arm by means of a gauge with diameter 27/64" (11 mm). (This gauge can be made from a rod about 3⅛" long). When the needle valve is closed, the needle valve arm should just contact the gauge.
4. If necessary, bend the arm where it joins the yoke-shape section in order to maintain the clearance mentioned in point 3 above.

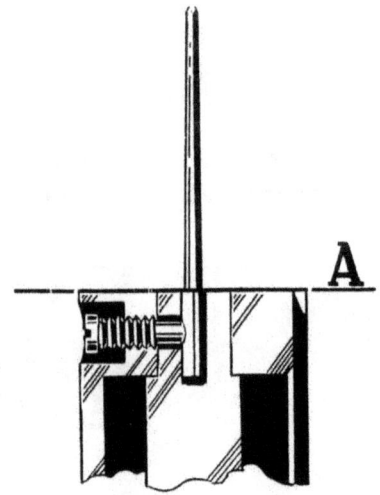

Fig. 88. Attachment of fuel needle (SU).

A = Attaching level

Replacement of fuel needle
1. Remove the suction chamber and the piston and fuel needle.
2. Loosen the screw on the fuel needle and pull out the fuel needle.
3. Fit a new fuel needle. Check that this is marked as mentioned in the Specifications. Push the needle so far into the piston that only the tapered working section is outside it. Tighten the lock screw.
4. Fit the parts into the **carburetor**. Then check that the piston

moves easily up and down. The piston can be lifted slightly without having to remove the air cleaner with the help of the pin. When the pin is slowly released, the piston should be heard to meet the bridge with a characteristic sound.

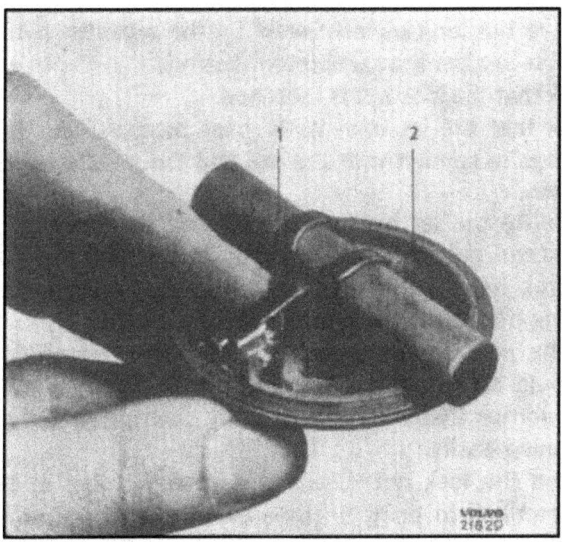

Fig. 89. Checking fuel level (SU).

1. Gauge (27/64" diameter)
2. Float bowl cover

Replacement of jet
1. Remove the jet as described under the heading "Disassembly and cleaning, jet unit." The adjuster nut does not need to be removed. If the carburetor is fitted on the engine the wire on the jet lever should be loosened.
2. Fit the new jet in the lower bearing and then fit the lower seal washer and packing, the spring, the upper seal washer with packing and the upper bearing with its copper washer. The brass washers for the upper and lower seals should be in contact with the spring.
3. Push in the jet together with the assembled parts into the carburetor housing. Screw on the lock nut loosely. Centralize the jet as shown below and then fit the lever and the other disassembled parts.

Centralizing the jet
In order to ensure that the carburetor functions in the correct way it is extremely important to make sure that the fuel needle moves easily up and down in the jet without jamming against

the walls of the jet. For this reason a very careful fit (centralizing) of the jet relative to the fuel needle is necessary.

The jet bearings are attached with quite a large lateral clearance so that they can be moved laterally when adjustment is carried out.

1. Remove the air cleaner. Screw up the adjuster nut as far as possible against the carburetor housing.
2. Check that the lock nut is loosened.
3. Check that the jet is in its highest position, i.e. that the jet heads is in contact with the nut and the needle is in its lower position.
4. Centralize the jet by carefully turning the lower jet bearing. Be careful not to disturb the adjuster nut. If the jet bearing requires moving slightly this can be carried out by slightly tapping the adjuster nut.
5. Lift the piston and the needle. When the piston is released it should strike against the bridge with a fully audible sound on condition that the jet is correctly centralized and the piston is running easily.
6. Tighten the lock nut. Check the pre-movement of the piston as described in point 5 above. Fit the air cleaner and make sure that the ventilation channels are not blocked.

Idling settings and the coupling together of the carburetors

Idling setting is carried out partly by means of the screws on the throttle arms which regulate engine speed, and partly by turning the adjuster nuts on the jet heads whereby the richness of the fuel mixture is altered. When the nuts are screwed down, a richer fuel mixture is obtained. If the nuts are screwed up the mixture will be leaner. The richness of the mixture is set during idling to cover the whole speed range of the engine.

When the correct idling speed has been obtained and both carburetors have been adjusted to the same level, they are then connected together. Individual settings should be carefully carried out before the carburetors are connected together in order to get the highest output for the engine.

1. Run the engine until it is thoroughly warmed up. If the jets have not been adjusted, a rough adjustment can be first carried out by screwing the adjuster nuts to their upper position and then screwing them down again one complete turn.
2. Loosen one of the couplings on the shaft between the carburetors. Make sure that the jets on both the carburetors are pressing against the adjuster nuts and that the screw for rapid idling is not in contact with the cam-shaped plate on each carburetor.

3. Adjust both throttles to the same position by screwing out the throttle adjuster screws and then screwing them in again until contact with the stop projections is just made. Then screw down each screw exactly one turn.
4. Start the engine. Check that the throttles are open to the same extent in both carburetors by listening to the sound with the aid of a rubber pipe placed in contact with the same point on the air cleaner of each carburetor. Adjust the idling screws until the air intake sound on both carburetors has exactly the same strength.
5. Adjust the jets by turning the adjuster nuts so that the idling speed is as high as possible with unchanged throttle opening. Adjust the carburetors one at a time. First screw the adjuster nuts upwards (leaner mixture) until the engine runs unevenly and then in the opposite direction until the engine runs perfectly smoothly. If the idling speed is too high it can be decreased by unscrewing the idling screws on the throttle shaft levers. Then check again as specified above that the air intake sound is equally strong on both carburetors.
6. Check that the fuel-air mixture is correct on both carburetors. First lift the piston on one of the carburetors slightly by means of the pin beside the air intake. Then release the pin and carry out the procedure on the other carburetor. The degree of uneven running on the engine should be the same in both cases. If the engine stalls when the piston on one of the carburetors is lifted, this usually means that the mixture on the other carburetor is too lean. The jet adjuster nut on the carburetor in question should be screwed carefully downwards to remedy this.
7. Connect the carburetors together by tightening the couplings on the shaft. Adjust the rapid idling screw. This is done by screwing the screw until it is in contact with the cam plate and then screwing it back until a certain clearance is obtained. Check once again that the air flow through both carburetors is the same. See point 4 above.

Rapid idling and control mechanism

The rapid idling system can be adjusted to suit varying conditions by means of the adjuster screw against the cam plate.

When the choke control is completely pushed in, the clearance between the adjuster screw and the cam plate should correspond to one turn of the screw.

AUTOBOOKS WORKSHOP MANUALS

ALFA ROMEO GIULIA 1300, 1600, 1750, 2000 1962-1978 WSM
BMW 1600 1966-1973 WSM
BMW 2000 & 2002 1966-1976 WSM
BMW 2500, 2800, 3.0 & 3.3 1968-1977 WSM
BMW 316, 320, 320i 1975-1977 WSM
BMW 518, 520, 520i 1973-1981 WSM
FIAT 1100, 1100D, 1100R & 1200 1957-1969 WSM
FIAT 124 1966-1974 WSM
FIAT 124 SPORT 1966-1975 WSM
FIAT 125 & 125 SPECIAL 1967-1973 WSM
FIAT 126, 126L, 126 DV, 126/650 & 126/650 DV 1972-1982 WSM
FIAT 127 SALOON, SPECIAL & SPORT, 900, 1050 1971-1981 WSM
FIAT 128 1969-1982 WSM
FIAT 1300, 1500 1961-1967 WSM
FIAT 131 MIRAFIORI 1975-1982 WSM
FIAT 132 1972-1982 WSM
FIAT 500 1957-1973 WSM
FIAT 600, 600D & MULTIPLA 1955-1969 WSM
FIAT 850 1964-1972 WSM
JAGUAR E-TYPE 1961-1972 WSM
JAGUAR MK 1, 2 1955-1969 WSM
JAGUAR S TYPE, 420 1963-1968 WSM
JAGUAR XK 120, 140, 150 MK 7, 8, 9 1948-1961 WSM
LAND ROVER 1, 2 1948-1961 WSM
MERCEDES-BENZ 190 1959-1968 WSM
MERCEDES-BENZ 220/8 1968-1972 WSM
MERCEDES-BENZ 220B 1959-1965 WSM
MERCEDES-BENZ 230 1963-1968 WSM
MERCEDES-BENZ 250 1968-1972 WSM
MERCEDES-BENZ 280 1968-1972 WSM
MG MIDGET TA-TF 1936-1955 WSM
MINI 1959-1980 WSM
MORRIS MINOR 1952-1971 WSM
PEUGEOT 404 1960-1975 WSM
PORSCHE 911 1964-1973 WSM
PORSCHE 911 1970-1977 WSM
RENAULT 16 1965-1979 WSM
RENAULT 8, 10, 1100 1962-1971 WSM
ROVER 3500, 3500S 1968-1976 WSM
SUNBEAM RAPIER, ALPINE 1955-1965 WSM
TRIUMPH SPITFIRE, GT6, VITESSE 1962-1968 WSM
TRIUMPH TR2, TR3, TR3A 1952-1962 WSM
TRIUMPH TR4, TR4A 1961-1967 WSM
VOLKSWAGEN BEETLE 1968-1977 WSM

VELOCEPRESS AUTOMOBILE BOOKS & MANUALS

ABARTH BUYERS GUIDE
AUSTIN-HEALEY 6-CYLINDER WSM
AUSTIN-HEALEY SPRITE & MG MIDGET 1958-1971 WSM
BMW 600 LIMOUSINE FACTORY WSM
BMW 600 LIMOUSINE OWNERS HAND BOOK & SERVICE MANUAL
BMW ISETTA FACTORY WSM
BOOK OF THE CARRERA PANAMERICANA - MEXICAN ROAD RACE
COMPLETE CATALOG OF JAPANESE MOTOR VEHICLES
CORVAIR 1960-1969 OWNERS WORKSHOP MANUAL
CORVETTE V8 1955-1962 OWNERS WORKSHOP MANUAL
DIALED IN - THE JAN OPPERMAN STORY
FERRARI 250/GT SERVICE AND MAINTENANCE
FERRARI 308 SERIES BUYER'S AND OWNER'S GUIDE
FERRARI BERLINETTA LUSSO
FERRARI BROCHURES AND SALES LITERATURE 1946-1967
FERRARI BROCHURES AND SALES LITERATURE 1968-1989
FERRARI GUIDE TO PERFORMANCE
FERRARI OPP, MAINTENANCE & SERVICE H/BOOKS 1948-1963
FERRARI OWNER'S HANDBOOK
FERRARI SERIAL NUMBERS PART I - ODD NUMBERS TO 21399
FERRARI SERIAL NUMBERS PART II - EVEN NUMBERS TO 1050
FERRARI SPYDER CALIFORNIA
FERRARI TUNING TIPS & MAINTENANCE TECHNIQUES
HENRY'S FABULOUS MODEL "A" FORD
HOW TO BUILD A FIBERGLASS CAR
HOW TO BUILD A RACING CAR
HOW TO RESTORE THE MODEL 'A' FORD
IF HEMINGWAY HAD WRITTEN A RACING NOVEL
JAGUAR E-TYPE 3.8 & 4.2 WSM
LE MANS 24 (THE BOOK THAT THE FILM WAS BASED ON)
MASERATI BROCHURES AND SALES LITERATURE
MASERATI OWNER'S HANDBOOK
METROPOLITAN FACTORY WSM
MGA & MGB OWNERS HANDBOOK & WSM
OBERT'S FIAT GUIDE
PERFORMANCE TUNING THE SUNBEAM TIGER
PORSCHE 356 1948-1965 WSM
PORSCHE 912 WSM
SOUPING THE VOLKSWAGEN
SU CARBURETORS (EMPHASIS ON UK AUTOMOBILES)
TRIUMPH TR2, TR3, TR4 1953-1965 WSM
TUNING FOR SPEED (P.E. IRVING)
VEDA ORR'S NEW REVISED HOT ROD PICTORIAL
VOLKSWAGEN TRANSPORTER, TRUCKS, STATION WAGONS WSM
VOLVO 1944-1968 ALL MODELS WSM
WEBER CARBURETORS (EMPHASIS ON ALFA & FIAT)

BROOKLANDS BOOKS & ROAD TEST PORTFOLIOS (RTP)

AC CARS 1904-2009
ALFA ROMEO 1920-1933 ROAD TEST PORTFOLIO
ALFA ROMEO 1934-1940 ROAD TEST PORTFOLIO
BRABHAM RALT HONDA THE RON TAURANAC STORY
BUGATTI TYPE 10 TO TYPE 40 ROAD TEST PORTFOLIO
BUGATTI TYPE 10 TO TYPE 251 ROAD TEST PORTFOLIO
BUGATTI TYPE 41 TO TYPE 55 ROAD TEST PORTFOLIO
BUGATTI TYPE 57 TO TYPE 251 ROAD TEST PORTFOLIO
DELAHAYE ROAD TEST PORTFOLIO
FERRARI ROAD CARS 1946-1956 ROAD TEST PORTFOLIO
FIAT 500 1936-1972 ROAD TEST PORTFOLIO
FIAT DINO ROAD TEST PORTFOLIO
HISPANO SUIZA ROAD TEST PORTFOLIO
HONDA ST1100/ST1300 PAN EUROPEAN 1990-2002 RTP
JAGUAR MK1 & MK2 ROAD TEST PORTFOLIO
LOTUS CORTINA ROAD TEST PORTFOLIO
MV AGUSTA F4 750 & 1000 1997-2007 ROAD TEST PORTFOLIO
TATRA CARS ROAD TEST PORTFOLIO

VELOCEPRESS MOTORCYCLE BOOKS & MANUALS

AJS SINGLES & TWINS 250cc THRU 1000cc 1932-1948 (BOOK OF)
AJS SINGLES 1955-65 350cc & 500cc (BOOK OF)
AJS SINGLES 1945-60 350cc & 500cc MODELS 16 & 18 (BOOK OF)
ARIEL 1939-1960 4 STROKE SINGLES (BOOK OF)
ARIEL LEADER & ARROW 1958-1964 (BOOK OF)
ARIEL MOTORCYCLES 1933-1951 WSM
ARIEL PREWAR MODELS 1932-1939 (BOOK OF)
BMW M/CYCLES R26 R27 (1956-1967) FACTORY WSM
BMW M/CYCLES R50 R50S R60 R69S (1955-1969) FACTORY WSM
BSA BANTAM (BOOK OF)
BSA ALL FOUR-STROKE SINGLES & V-TWINS 1936-1952 (BOOK OF)
BSA OHV & SV SINGLES - 250cc 1954-1970 (BOOK OF)
BSA OHV & SV SINGLES 1945-54 250-600cc (BOOK OF)
BSA OHV SINGLES 350 & 500cc 1955-1967 (BOOK OF)
BSA PRE-WAR MODELS TO 1939 (BOOK OF)
BSA TWINS 1948-1962 (BOOK OF)
BSA TWINS 1962-1969 (SECOND BOOK OF)
CATALOG OF BRITISH MOTORCYCLES (1951 MODELS)
DOUGLAS PRE-WAR ALL MODELS 1929-1939 (BOOK OF)
DOUGLAS POST-WAR ALL MODELS 1948-1957 FACTORY WSM
DUCATI 160cc, 250cc & 350cc OHC MODELS FACTORY WSM
HONDA 50 ALL MODELS UP TO 1970 INC MONKEY & TRAIL (BOOK OF)
HONDA 90 ALL MODELS UP TO 1966 (BOOK OF)
HONDA MOTORCYCLES 125-150 TWINS C/CS/CB/CA WSM
HONDA MOTORCYCLES 250-305 TWINS C/CS/CB WSM
HONDA MOTORCYCLES C100 SUPER CUB WSM
HONDA MOTORCYCLES C110 SPORT CUB 1962-1969 WSM
HONDA TWINS & SINGLES 50cc THRU 305cc 1960-1966 (BOOK OF)
HONDA TWINS ALL MODELS 125cc THRU 450cc UP TO 1968 (BOOK OF)
INDIAN PONYBIKE, BOY RACER & PAPOOSE ILL PARTS LIST & SALES LIT
J.A.P. ENGINES 1927-1952 & MOTORCYCLES 1934-1952 (BOOK OF)
LAMBRETTA ALL 125 & 150cc MODELS 1947-1957 (BOOK OF)
LAMBRETTA LI & TV MODELS 1957-1970 (SECOND BOOK OF)
MATCHLESS 350 & 500cc SINGLES 1945-1956 (BOOK OF)
MATCHLESS 350 & 500cc SINGLES 1955-1966 (BOOK OF)
NORTON 1932-1947 (BOOK OF)
NORTON 1938-1956 (BOOK OF)
NORTON DOMINATOR TWINS 1955-1965 (BOOK OF)
NORTON MODELS 19, 50 & ES2 1955-1963 (BOOK OF)
NORTON MOTORCYCLES 1957-1970 FACTORY WSM
NORTON PREWAR MODELS 1932-1939 (BOOK OF)
NSU PRIMA ALL MODELS 1956-1964 (BOOK OF)
NSU QUICKLY ALL MODELS 1953-1963 (BOOK OF)
RALEIGH MOPEDS 1960-1969 (BOOK OF)
ROYAL ENFIELD SINGLES & V TWINS 1937-1953 (BOOK OF)
ROYAL ENFIELD SINGLES 1946-1962 (BOOK OF)
ROYAL ENFIELD 736cc INTERCEPTOR FACTORY WSM
ROYAL ENFIELD 250cc & 350cc SINGLES 1958-1966 (SECOND BOOK OF)
SUNBEAM MOTORCYCLES 1928-1939 (BOOK OF)
SUNBEAM S7 & S8 1946-1957 (BOOK OF)
SUZUKI 50cc & 80cc UP TO 1966 (BOOK OF)
SUZUKI T10 1963-1967 FACTORY WSM
SUZUKI T20 & T200 1965-1969 FACTORY WSM
TRIUMPH PRE-WAR MOTORCYCLE 1935-1939 (BOOK OF)
TRIUMPH MOTORCYCLES 1935-1949 (BOOK OF)
TRIUMPH MOTORCYCLES 1937-1951 WSM
TRIUMPH MOTORCYCLES 1945-1955 FACTORY WSM
TRIUMPH TWINS 1945-1958 (BOOK OF)
TRIUMPH TWINS 1956-1969 (BOOK OF)
VELOCETTE ALL SINGLES & TWINS 1925-1970 (BOOK OF)
VESPA 1951-1961 (BOOK OF)
VESPA 125 & 150cc & GS MODELS 1955-1963 (SECOND BOOK OF)
VESPA 125 & 150cc 1963-1972 (THIRD BOOK OF)
VESPA GS & SS 1955-1968 (BOOK OF)
VILLIERS ENGINE (BOOK OF)
VINCENT MOTORCYCLES 1935-1955 WSM

PLEASE VISIT OUR WEBSITE
www.VelocePress.com
FOR A DETAILED DESCRIPTION
OF ANY OF THESE TITLES

www.ingramcontent.com/pod-product-compliance
Lightning Source LLC
Chambersburg PA
CBHW070544170426
43200CB00011B/2540